© 2022 North Parade Publishing Ltd.
Published by North Parade Publishing Ltd.
3-6 Henrietta Mews, Bath, England.
BA2 6LR

Printed in China

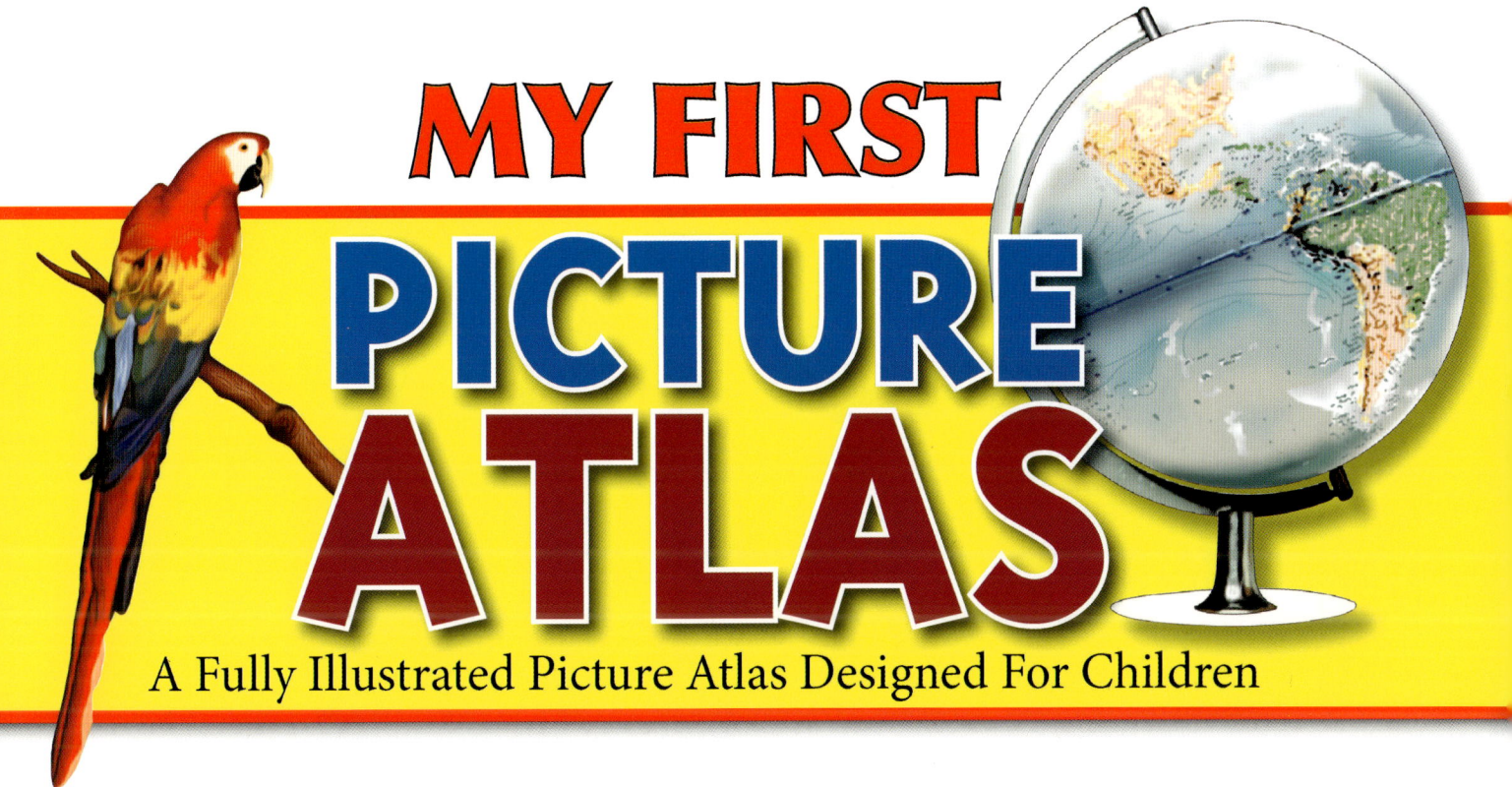

MY FIRST
PICTURE
ATLAS

A Fully Illustrated Picture Atlas Designed For Children

CONTENTS

Introduction

The Polar Regions

North America   22

World Map

The World Map shows us the continents of North America, South America, Europe, Asia, Africa, Australia, and Antarctica. Within the continents are different countries. The world's largest country is the Russian Federation, and the smallest is the Vatican City. Water covers two-thirds of the world. The oceans hold most of this water; they are the Pacific, the Atlantic, the Indian, the Arctic and the Southern Ocean. Other important water bodies include lakes and rivers inland.

Latitude and Longitude

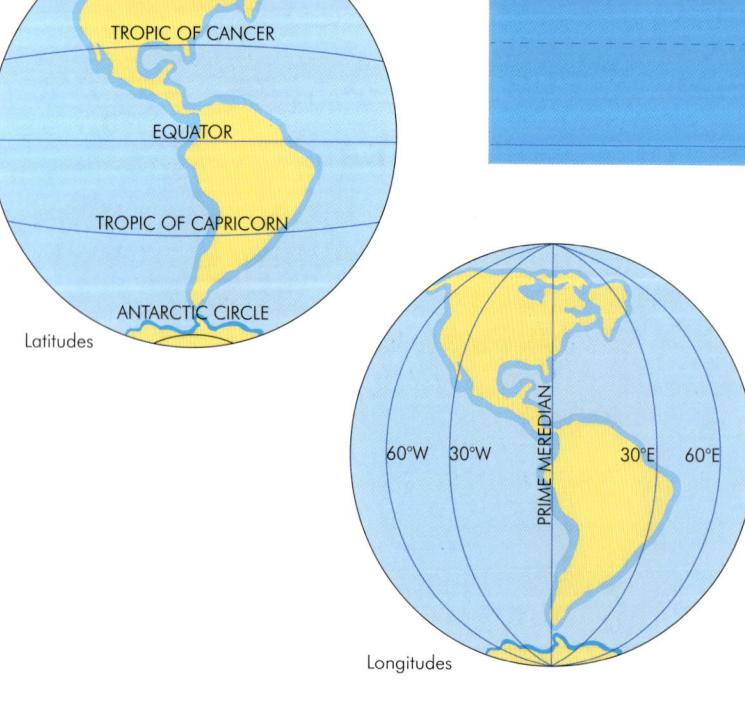

Latitudes

Longitudes

A globe shows what the Earth looks like from a great distance. Lands, oceans, mountains, rivers, countries and cities are all shown on the globe. It is marked with a grid of imaginary lines, called the lines of latitude and longitude. Lines of longitude run from north to south. The lines of latitude circle the globe horizontally. The line of latitude that runs around the middle of the Earth, the widest portion, is called the Equator. The lines of longitude divide the earth through its poles, like the green lines on a watermelon. A map-reader can easily find any place on the globe by using these lines.

C O C E A N

ARCTIC CIRCLE

GREENLAND
(DENMARK)

ICELAND

Svalbard
(NORWAY)

Novaya
Zemlya

Faeroe Islands
(DENMARK)

RUSSIAN FEDERATION

IRELAND
UNITED
KINGDOM

NORWAY
SWEDEN
FINLAND

DENMARK
BALTIC
SEA
35

GERMANY
POLAND
BELARUS

FRANCE
UKRAINE

KAZAKHSTAN

MONGOLIA

Kuril Islands
(RUSSIA)

Azores
(PORTUGAL)

PORTUGAL
SPAIN

ROMANIA

BLACK SEA

CASPIAN SEA

UZBEKISTAN
KYRGYZSTAN

NORTH
KOREA

JAPAN

Madeira
(PORTUGAL)

Gibraltar
(UK)

MOROCCO

TUNISIA
MEDITERRANEAN SEA
MALTA

GREECE
TURKEY

CYPRUS
LEBANON
ISRAEL
SYRIA
IRAQ

TURKMENISTAN
TAJIKISTAN

AFGHANISTAN

IRAN

CHINA

SOUTH
KOREA

PACIFIC OCEAN

TROPIC OF CANCER

Wake Island
(USA)

Canary
Islands
(SPAIN)

WESTERN
SAHARA

ALGERIA

LIBYA

EGYPT

JORDAN
KUWAIT

SAUDI
ARABIA

PAKISTAN

NEPAL
BHUTAN

INDIA

BANGLADESH

BURMA
(MYANMAR)
(LAOS)

Northern
Mariana
Islands (USA)

Guam
(USA)

Marshall
Islands

Cape
Verde

MAURITANIA

MALI

NIGER

CHAD

SUDAN

RED SEA

ERITREA

YEMEN

OMAN

THAILAND

CAMBODIA

VIETNAM

PALAU

MICRONESIA

SENEGAL
GAMBIA
GUINEA-BISSAU
GUINEA
SIERRA LEONE
LIBERIA

BURKINA
FASO

BENIN
NIGERIA

IVORY
COAST
GHANA

CENTRAL
AFRICAN
REPUBLIC

CAMEROON

SOUTH
SUDAN

ETHIOPIA

DJIBOUTI

SOMALIA

Lakshadweep
(INDIA)

MALDIVES

SRI
LANKA

Andaman
(INDIA)

Nicobar
(INDIA)

BRUNEI

MALAYSIA
SINGAPORE

EQUATOR

EQUATOR

EQUATOR

NAURU

KIRIBATI

EQUATORIAL
GUINEA
SAO TOME
& PRINCIPE

GABON
CONGO

DEM. REP. OF
CONGO
(ZAIRE)

UGANDA
RWANDA
BURUNDI

KENYA

TANZANIA

SEYCHELLES

Diego Garcia

INDONESIA

PAPUA
NEW GUINEA

EAST TIMOR

SOLOMON
ISLANDS

TUVALU

ANGOLA

ZAMBIA

COMOROS

MADAGASCAR

MAURITIUS

Reunion
(FRANCE)

INDIAN OCEAN

Cocos Island
(AUSTRALIA)

Christmas
Island
(AUSTRALIA)

Coral Sea
Islands
Territory
(AUSTRALIA)

VANUATU

New
Caledonia
(FRANCE)

FIJI

ZIMBABWE

NAMIBIA

BOTSWANA

MOZAMBIQUE

SWAZILAND

LESOTHO
SOUTH
AFRICA

TROPIC OF CAPRICORN

AUSTRALIA

Iles Kerguelen
(FRANCE)

Tasmania

NEW
ZEALAND

Georgia (UK)

ANTARCTIC CIRCLE

ANTARCTICA

How to Draw a Map

As the Earth is round, its surface has to
be flattened out to show it on the page.
Imagine the watermelon with the map of
the Earth drawn on it. To flatten the melon,
it would have to be cut in sections along
the green lines. To use this map would be
difficult. To draw a flat map, parts of the
world have to be stretched. This way of
drawing a map is known as projection.
No map that is drawn this way can be
absolutely accurate, whereas a globe is
exactly the way the Earth is.

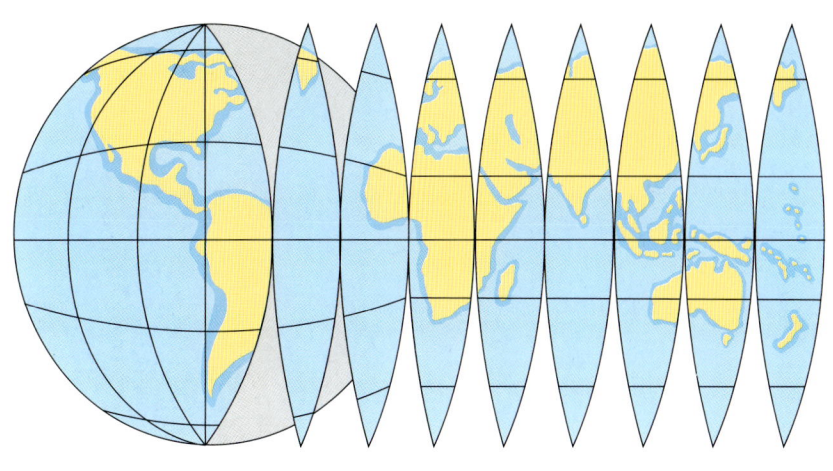

Our Planet

It is commonly believed that the Earth was formed more than 4.6 billion years ago, when there was an enormous explosion from a spinning cloud of gases and dust - this is known as the Big Bang theory. The sun and the planets were also formed at the same time. To begin with, the planets were very hot, then they cooled down. Life began about 3,500 million years ago. At first it was only microscopic bacteria and algae, that grew in water bodies. Then plants appeared, after which jellyfish-like creatures appeared in the sea. Mammals and humans came much later.

Atmosphere

When seen from space, the Earth looks like a blue ball, surrounded by swirls of clouds. We know this from pictures sent back by satellites. Two third of the Earth's surface is covered with water. It is surrounded by a blanket of gases called the atmosphere, which stretches to about 10,000 km in space.

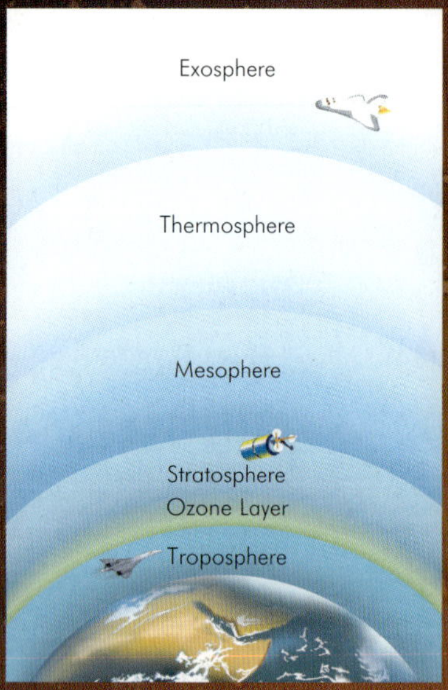

Exosphere

Thermosphere

Mesosphere

Stratosphere
Ozone Layer

Troposphere

Solar System

The solar system is made up of nine planets, each of which orbits a huge, hot and shining star – the Sun. Earth is not only one of the smaller planets, it is the only one with water and oxygen, required for us to live. Mercury and Venus are hot, while Mars, Jupiter, Saturn, Uranus and Neptune are very cold.

Mercury

Venus

Earth

Mars

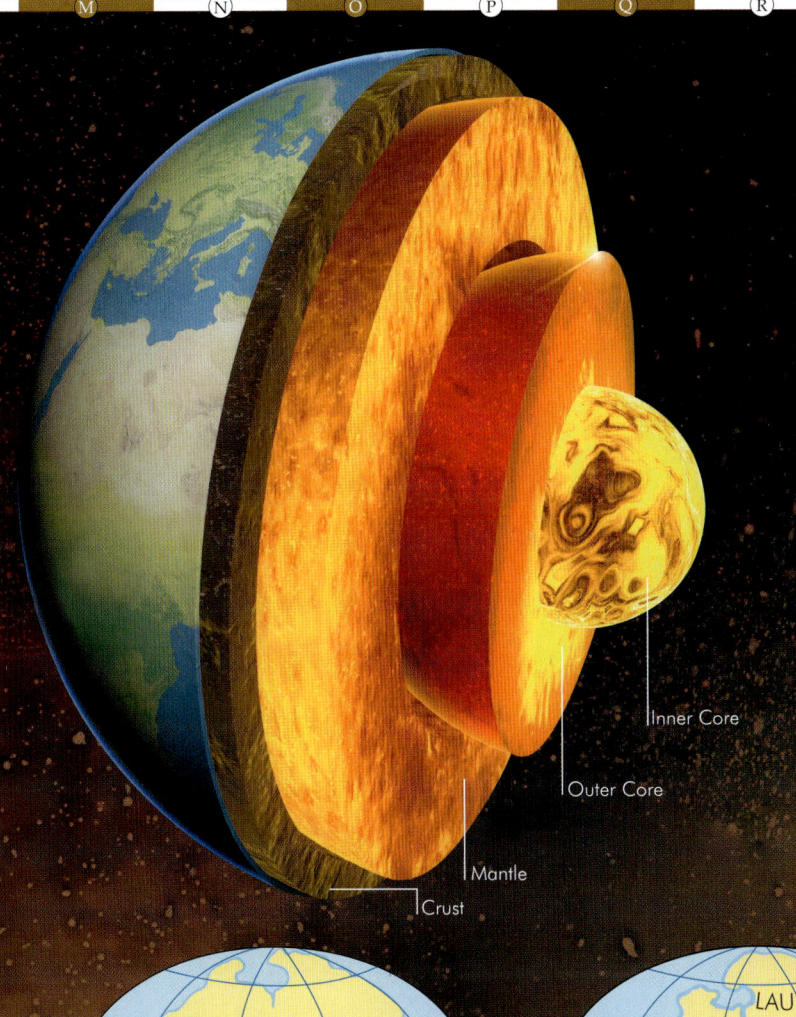

Inside the Earth

We live on the crust, or the outer part of the Earth, which is made up of hard rocks, covered with water in places. Below lies a mantle of hot rock. Below that is a magnetic mass of molten metal, or the outer core. The very heart of the Earth - a hot solid mix of iron and nickel - is called the inner core.

Inner Core

Outer Core

Mantle

Crust

Continental Drift

In the beginning, the Earth looked very different. The continents and the oceans have changed their positions since then. This movement is called continental drift. About 250 million years ago, all the land on Earth was joined together as one supercontinent called Pangaea. This split some 100 million years later into two land masses, Laurasia and Gondwanaland. Laurasia consisted of North America, Europe and a part of Asia. Gondwanaland included South America, Africa, India, Australia and Antarctica. The drift continued. Since then the continents have slowly drifted to their present positions.

Pangaea, when all the continents were joined together 200 million years ago

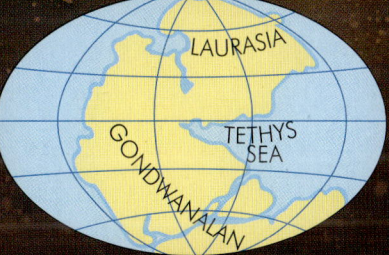

About a 100 million years ago

Today, when the continents have drifted to their present positions

Jupiter

Saturn

Uranus

Neptune

The Earth: Time and Seasons

The Earth spins like a top around its own axis. At the same time, it revolves around the Sun. These movements give us day and night and the seasons.

Day and Night

The Earth spins around its own axis. It takes 23 hours, 56 minutes and 4 seconds to complete a full circle. As it spins, the side that faces the sun has daylight. The side that is away experiences night. If you were to hold a ball in front of a lamp, and turn the ball round slowly, you would see that at all times only one half of the ball receives light. Since the Earth spins eastward, the sun seems to rise in the east.

SUN'S RAYS

NORTH POLE

DAY

NIGHT

SOUTH POLE

21st March is when spring begins in the Northern Hemisphere and autumn in the Southern Hemisphere.

21st June is when summer begins in the Northern Hemisphere and winter in the Southern Hemisphere.

21st or 22nd June is the longest day of the year in the Northern Hemisphere and the shortest day in the Southern Hemisphere.

23rd September is when autumn begins in the Northern Hemisphere and spring begins in the Southern Hemisphere.

The Year

The Earth also circles the Sun. The path of the Earth around the Sun is called an orbit. It takes the Earth one year, or 365.26 days, to complete its journey around the Sun. The Earth covers a distance of 958 million kilometres in one revolution. It travels at an average speed of about 30 kilometres per second.

The Seasons

The axis of the Earth is at an angle to the plane of its orbit. It is tilted by 23.45 degrees. As the Earth journeys around the Sun, the places that are tilted towards the Sun receive more light and heat. In other words, they have a summer season. The places that are tilted away from the sun have less sunlight and experience winter.

The Force of Gravity

Gravity is the force - or the pull of attraction - that all bodies in the Universe exert on all other bodies. Because of the force of gravity, the Earth and all the other eight planets, each with its own orbit, circle around the Sun. Bodies with greater masses have a greater force of attraction or gravitational pull. The further away they are from each other, the lesser the attracting force.

21st December is when winter begins in the Northern Hemisphere and summer begins in the Southern Hemisphere.

Moon's Orbit

Moon and Earth

The Moon is the Earth's own satellite. It is a ball of rock, about a quarter of the size of the Earth. It has no atmosphere, water, or life. The Moon is pitted with craters and has flat plains and jagged mountain ranges. The surface is made of rocks and fine dust.

The gravity of the Earth pulls the Moon towards it. This makes the Moon orbit the Earth. It takes 28 days, or one lunar month, to circle the Earth. In turn, the force of the Moon's gravity on the Earth pulls upon water in the oceans and the seas. This creates a bulge in the water. As the Earth rotates, the bulge shifts from east to west, twice a day. This shifting of water creates tides.

Weather

Rain, sunshine, snow, gales and balmy breezes: all make up the weather of a place. All these happen in the lower layer of the Earth's atmosphere. The atmosphere is affected by wind, water and the Sun.

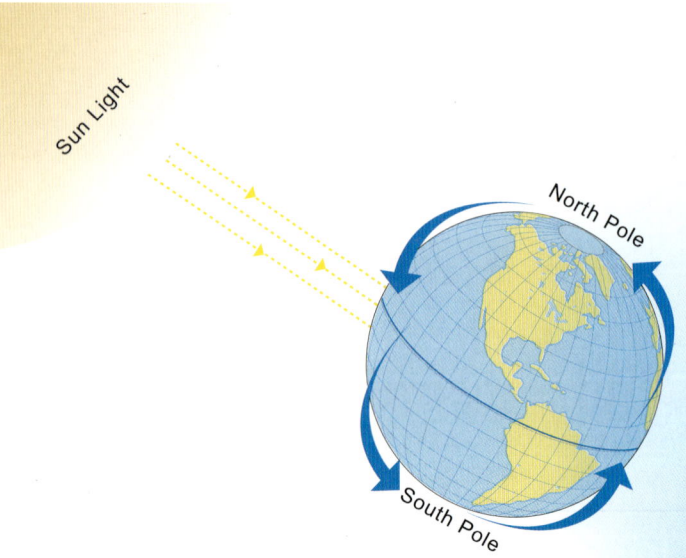

Wind

At the Equator, the air warmed by the Sun rises and moves. Drier and colder air from the higher latitudes moves in. Thus, there is a constant movement of air. Huge masses of cold and hot air flow between the tropics and the polar regions. When air masses meet, rise and fall, or heat and cool, the changes that take place create weather. This is a constant process.

Sunny Day

The sun shines bright and the air is warm. Sometimes a few wispy clouds can float about for a little while. In the winter, it can be cold on a sunny day.

Types of Wind

Gentle breeze: Kites fly and flags flutter

Strong wind: Difficult to control umbrellas

Gale: Large trees sway and bend over

Storm: Trees uprooted

How Clouds Form

When the air gets warm, the water vapour in it rises. It cools and condenses into tiny droplets, which join together to form clouds. When the droplets in the clouds become heavy, they fall as rain. High clouds are made of ice crystals and the lower ones of water droplets.

Types of Clouds

Cirrus
Highest, wispy cloud found at 5,000 - 13,000m

Cumulonimbus
Huge, flat-topped, storm clouds found at 15,000m

Cumulus
Puffyclouds with grey bases and white tops

Stratus
Lowest clouds found at 2000m

RAINBOW
When sunlight passes through a raindrop, it splits into different colours - red, orange, yellow, green, blue, indigo and violet. Red is always at the top.

HAIL
Hailstones are round pellets of ice that are formed inside a cloud. Raindrops within a cloud freeze when they are carried higher up by air currents.

SNOW
When a tiny water droplet freezes in a cloud, it binds together into a flat, six-sided crystal. Between 2 and 2,000 crystals make one snowflake. No two snowflakes are alike.

Cloudy Day

Clouds hover across the sky and it might rain. Sometimes thick clouds move away for a short while to let in a little sunshine.

Lightning

Lightning is a spark of electricity that is caused in a storm cloud when electrical charges build up. The air is heated rapidly, creating thunder.

Hurricane

Hurricanes are massive storms that form over tropical waters in the oceans, causing great devastation when they strike land. Typhoons and cyclones are violent storms too.

Tornado

A tornado is a twisting storm funnel, carrying winds that can reach up to 350 km/h. Tornadoes can measure a few hundred meters wide.

WEATHER CHART		
	☀	Sunshine
	☁	Cloud
	⛅	Overcast Cloud
	🌧	Rain Cloud

Biomes: Climate Zones

Climate is the weather of an area over a long period of time. A place can have a wet, dry, cold, hot, or moderate climate. The conditions that affect climate include sunshine, temperature, rainfall, humidity, ocean currents and the 'greenhouse effect'. The location of a place on the globe also affects its climate. The Earth can be divided into regions with similar climates. The climate determines the kind of plants growing in an area. When a similar type of vegetation grows over a vast area, it is called a biome.

Grassland

Grasslands are dry regions marked by an annual rainy season. The rain helps the plants and grasses grow, turning the land into a green scenery. Grassland vegetation is mostly made up of grasses and trees that do not need much water. All over the world, grasslands are cultivated or used for pasture and cattle ranching.

Tropical Rainforest

Tropical rainforests are found in hot and rainy places, on either side of the equator. Trees grow very tall, reaching up to about 40 metres. The tops of these trees merge to form a canopy, shading the ground. The variety of plant and animal species is greater here than in any other type of forest.

Desert

Deserts are sandy, stormy regions with little or no rainfall. Deserts experience the hottest climates in the world. There are hardly any plants. Only shrubs, thorny trees, cacti and water storing acacias grow here.

Temperate Forest

Temperate forests have deciduous trees that shed their leaves once a year, either in the winter or in the dry season. Broad-leaved trees like oak, maple, beech and chestnut are found here. Their leaves change to yellow, red and, finally, brown.

Coniferous Forest

Cold climates have evergreen coniferous forests of pine and fir. These trees can grow in snowy areas and mountain slopes. The taiga region in Eurasia has the world's largest coniferous forest.

Tundra

The Tundra is a vast, frozen treeless plain. It is the belt just below the Arctic circle, spread all across the northern continents. The polar regions are icebound the year round, with freezing temperatures.

GLOBAL WARMING

DEFORESTATION

All over the world tropical rainforests are being cut down at an alarming rate, for timber, ranches and farmland. Plant and animal species are disappearing.

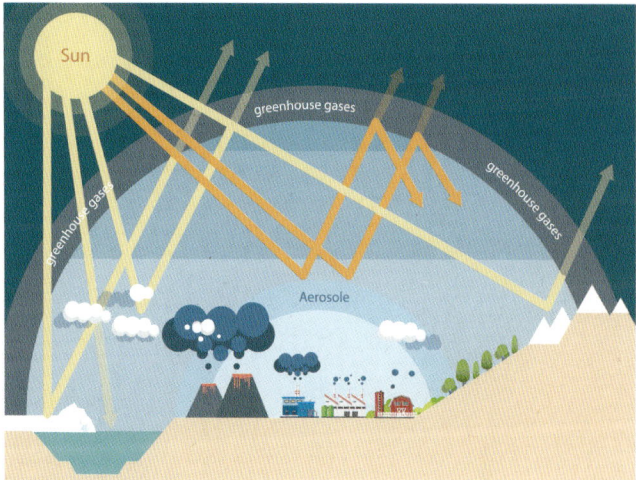

GREENHOUSE EFFECT

The oceans and the land absorb a large amount of the sun's heat. Some of this heat is reflected back into space. The Earth's atmosphere has gases that stop much of the heat from escaping, this keeps the Earth warm. By burning fossil fuels and cutting down forests, we release larger and larger amounts of these greenhouse gases into the atmosphere. Because of this the Earth is warming up slowly. This is called global warming.

POLLUTION

Cars, factories and power stations pump waste gases into the air. Coal, oil and petrol, when burnt for energy, all create gases which dissolve in the atmosphere to form acids. Later they fall back to the Earth as acid rain, sometimes hundreds of kilometers away from where they were formed.

Acid rain is harmful for trees, plants and crops and it kills fish in lakes and rivers.

Land and Water

Plateau

A plateau is a broad, flat-topped mountain with steep sides. It is usually formed when magma under the Earth's crust slowly pushes up large, flat areas of land.

Volcanoes

Volcanoes are formed when openings in the Earth's crust spew out hot, molten rock, or magma. Some volcanoes explode violently, hurling hot gases and ash upwards. Others erupt quietly. The liquid rock, or lava, cools around the openings in cone-shaped forms. Volcanoes occur on mountain ranges, land and even ocean beds. A volcano that erupts often is called an active volcano.

Mountain

A mountain is formed when parts of the Earth's crust collide. As these parts crumple and fold, the rock and the sediments between them get pushed to a great height.

Waterfall

When a river drops over a cliff with great force, a waterfall is created.

River

A river originates as a small stream from glaciers and springs. As it flows downhill, it is fed by rain and snow. The river then broadens out.

Lake

A lake is a large hollow of still water. Inflowing streams and underground springs fill a lake.

Sea and Ocean

A river's journey ends at the sea, which eventually merges into an ocean.

How to Use This Atlas

The Atlas is split into sections based on the continents:
Antarctica, North America, South America, Europe, Africa,
Asia and Australasia. Each section starts with a map of
the continent, such as the Africa map shown below. The
continents are further divided into regions, which are
illustrated in the regional maps that follow.

Fact Files

Each continent has a
fact box that highlights
its unique features. This
could be the longest
river or the highest
mountain in the region.

The Location

The area marked in
brown helps you
identify where the
region is located.

Regional Map

All the important
cities and capitals
are marked. It also
shows the animals,
plants, crops,
industries and
natural resources
specific to the region.

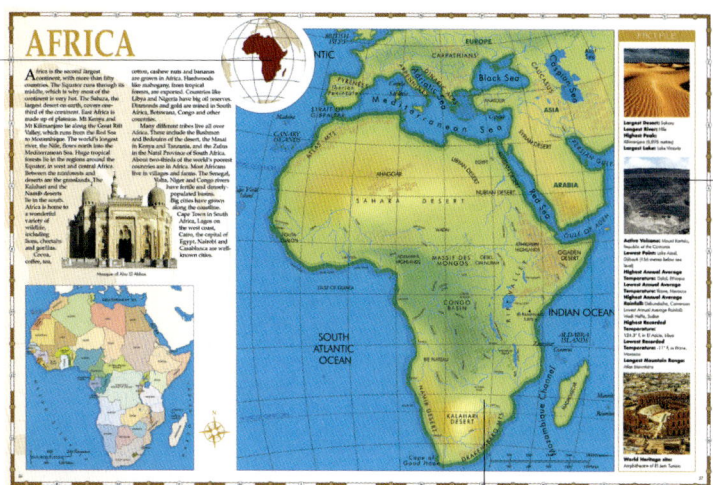

Grid

To look for a
particular place in
the atlas, look it up
in the index. Beside
the name of the
place, you will see a
page number
followed by a letter
and a number.
Trace along the grid
number of the page.
Then look for the
corresponding letter.
The place is located
where the
two lines meet.

Geographical Map

This map shows the
major mountains,
deserts, rivers, lakes
and the oceans.

Special Features

Each region has feature
boxes that include such
things as an important
plant, animal, landmarks,
fairs and festivals.

Scale

Each map has a scale.
This shows how large a
continent or country is.

Political Map

This map shows
all the independent
countries within a
continent.

KEYS TO THE MAP

Capital City	City	Country Name	Mountains	River	Wheat	Cotton	Industry	Mine	Mountain Peak	Timber
London	Norwich	ITALY	ALPS MTS	THAMES	🌾	🌿	🏭	🛒	MT ELBERT	🪵

ARCTIC

An imaginary line called the Arctic Circle runs along the northern part of the Earth. The Arctic Ocean and the land that borders it falls within the Arctic Circle. Around the North Pole the Arctic is frozen all the year round. Unlike the Antarctic, there is no land under the ice cap. The ice often breaks up to form floes and icebergs, which float in the surrounding oceans.

The northernmost part of Scandinavia, Russia, Alaska, Canada and Greenland touch the Arctic Ocean. The frozen tundra plains run all along the coastline. The tundra has a very short summer, when the land thaws and flowers and mosses grow. Many birds come to breed. Since the sun does not set on some days in the summer, the Arctic is known as the Land of the Midnight Sun. While the musk ox, reindeer, Arctic hare and the Arctic tern migrate to the south during winters, the polar bear stay on to hunt seals and catch fish in the icy water. Coal, iron and oil are found in the Arctic.

FACT FILE

First Expedition:
Robert E. Peary, April 1909
Highest Point:
Mt Gunnbjorn, Greenland (3,700 metres)
Lowest Point:
Fram Basin (4,665 metres deep)
Lowest Temperature:
-70° C, recorded at Nord station, Greenland

ATLANTIC OCEAN

Chukchi Sea

East Siberian Sea

Killer whales

Natural gas

Walruses

Beluga white whale

Oil

LIMIT OF PARMANENT PACK ICE

Puffins

Arctic hare

Arctic terns

Snow geese

Beluga white whale

Beaufort Sea

Red fox

ARCTIC OCEAN

Polar bears

AVERAGE PERMANENT EXTENT OF SEA ICE

Banks Island

Musk ox

Skua

Walruses

Lemming

Oil

Natural gas

North Pole

Kara Sea

Queen Elizabeth Islands

Arctic camping

Ellesmere Island

Narwhal

Arctic white fox

Baffin Island

Arctic white fox

Arctic terns

Reindeer

Ice-breaker ship

Coal

Polar bears

Natural gas

Barents Sea

DAVIS STRAIT

BAFFIN BAY

Puffins

Oil

SVALBARD ISLANDS

Norwegian Sea

Harp seals

Arctic white fox

Walruses

Fishing trawler

Greenland Sea

Hooded seals

Walruses

Musk ox

Killer whales

Humpback whales

Iceland

ATLANTIC OCEAN

| 0 | 350 | 700 | 1050 | 1400 | 1750 Kilometres |
| 0 | 200 | 400 | 600 | 800 | 1000 Miles |

FLORA AND FAUNA

When the snow melts in the short summer, many flowers bloom. The Arctic Poppy rotates with the sun and collects sunlight. This flower attracts many insects.

Polar bears are strong swimmers who hunt along the Arctic shelves for seals and fish. Their white coats blend into the icy landscape as they stalk their prey. The hollow hairs of their fur trap air to keep them warm.

FLORA AND FAUNA

Huge groups of up to 6,000 Emperor penguins can be seen huddling together to be warm. One of six penguin species that breed in Antarctica, these birds have dense feathers and fat stores that help them stay warm.

Due to the bitter cold of winter, nothing grows in Antarctica. In the very brief summer lichens, mosses, algae, fungi and liverworts grow in the cracks and crevices of rocks.

ANTARCTIC

The frozen continent of Antarctica is located around the South Pole. This is a land of mountains and glaciers. Most of the land remains permanently buried under ice sheets. In places, the ice can be almost 2,100 metres thick. This thickness of the ice sheet makes Antarctica the continent with the highest average altitude.

The continent is divided in two parts by the 3,200-kilometre long Trans-Antarctic Mountains, which contain an active volcano, Mt Erebus. The ice slowly flows down to the shores and spreads out over the sea, creating massive ice shelves. When the shelf becomes too heavy, it breaks off to form huge glaciers that float through the southern ocean. The world's largest glacier, the Lambert glacier is in the Australian Antarctic territory. It is nearly 400 kilometres long and about 40 kilometres wide. This continent is the coldest and windiest spot on the planet. The lowest temperature on Earth, -128.6 degree Fahreinheit, was recorded here. Penguins, albatrosses and seals live around the coast. Baleen whales, seals and fish live in the surrounding ocean. No humans, except for visiting scientists, live here.

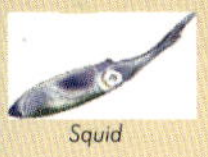

Map labels

SOUTH ATLANTIC OCEAN

Bellingshausen Sea

Weddell Sea

Queen Maud Land

Kelp gull

Blue whales

Leopard seal

Fur seals

Octopus

Seals

Squid

Cormorant

ANTARCTIC PENINSULA

Emperor penguins

Skua

Adelie penguins

RONNE ICE SHELF

Elephant seal

Blue whales

Sheathbill

Adelie penguins

Antarctic terns

Albatross

Cormorant

Antarctic snow petrels

Squid

PRYDZ BAY

Davis Sea

ANTARCTICA

● South Pole

TRANS-ANTARCTIC MTS

MARIE BYRD LAND

Emperor penguins

ROSS ICE SHELF

South pole station

Squid

Leopard seal

Emperor penguins

Krill

Ice-breaker ship

Fur seals

Natural gas

Coal

Oil

Seals

Skua

Adelie penguins

SOUTH PACIFIC OCEAN

WILKES LAND

Fur seals

Sei whales

INDIAN OCEAN

Amundsen Sea

Squid

N

Scale: 0 600 1200 1800 2400 Kilometres
0 300 600 900 1200 Miles

FACT FILE

Tallest Mountain Range: Ellsworth Mountains

Highest Point: Vinson Massif (4,892 metres)

Lowest Point: Bentley Subglacial Trench (-2,555 metres)

Lowest Temperature: -128.6° F, in Vostok

Highest Temperature: 59° F, in Vanda Station, Scott Coast

Largest Ice Shelf: Ross Ice Shelf

Active Volcano: Mount Erebus

Land Mass: 14.2 million square kilometres

Maximum Known Thickness of Ice: 2,100 metres

NORTH AMERICA

North America is the third largest continent in the world. It includes Canada, the United States, Mexico, the countries of Central America and the islands of the Caribbean. The continent stretches from the Arctic Circle to 500 miles short of the Equator. Mexico and the Central American countries lie in the southern part. In the north is the ice-capped Greenland. It is the world's largest island. The landscape varies from rugged mountains to flat plains. In the west are the Rocky Mountains and in the east is the Appalachian range. The frozen tundra lies to the north. Barren and hot deserts are found towards the southwest. Panama and Nicaragua lie in the narrow ribbon of land that links North America to South America. It is believed that the first people of America came from Asia. Then came the native Americans, who have lived in North America for thousands of years. The ruins of the Mayan and Aztec civilisations are found here. Immigrants from Africa and Europe began moving to America in the 1600s. Canada and the United States are among the most industrialised countries. Some of the world's largest cities including New York, Los Angeles, Chicago and Mexico City are found in this continent.

1. ST KITTS & NEVIS
2. ANTIGUA & BARBUDA
3. DOMINICA
4. ST LUCIA
5. ST VINCENT & THE GRENADINES
6. BARBADOS
7. GRENADA
8. TRINIDAD & TOBAGO

ARCTIC OCEAN

ICELAND

GREENLAND

aufort Sea

Banks Island

BAFFIN BAY

ARCTIC CIRCLE

DAVIS STRAIT

Victoria Island

Ellesmere Island

BAFFIN ISLANDS

MACKENZIE

GREAT BEAR LAKE

Labrador Sea

BACK

LIARD

GREAT SLAVE LAKE

DUBAWNT

Labrador
Peninsula

PEACE

HUDSON BAY

Newfoundland
Island

LAKE ATHABASCA

CANADIAN SHIELD

NELSON

SASKATCHEWAN

LAKE WINNIPEG

EASTMAIN

LAURENTIAN PLATEAU

ST LAWRENCE

GULF OF LAWRENCE

G R E A T

LAKE MANITOBA

MISSOURI

GREAT LAKES

NOVA SCOTIA

R O C K Y

P L A I N S

LAKE MICHIGAN

LAKE ERIE

APPALACHIAN MTS

SNAKE

PLATTE

MISSISSIPPI

MISSOURI

OHIO

M T S

GREAT
BASIN

TENNESSEE

NORTH ATLANTIC
OCEAN

ADA

RED

ALABAMA

COASTAL PLAINS

Sargasso
Sea

GULF OF CALIFORNIA

WESTERN SIERRA MADRE

RIO GRANDE

FLORIDA STRAIT

EASTERN SIERRA MADRE

GULF OF
MEXICO

SANTIAGO

CUBA

GREATER ANTILLES

Caribbean
Sea

BALSAS

GULF OF
HONDURAS

COCO

ANDES

GULF OF

0	500	1000	1500	2000 Kilometres
0	250	500	750	1000 1250 Miles

FACT FILE

Highest Peak:
Mount McKinley (6,190
metres)
Longest River: Mississippi-
Missouri river system
Largest Desert:
Great Basin, USA
**Largest Freshwater
Lake:** Lake Superior
Active Volcano:
Mount St Helens, USA
Lowest Point:
Death Valley, USA
**Lowest Recorded
Temperature:** -93.2°F,
in Northice, Greenland
**Highest Recorded
Temperature:** 134°F, in
Death Valley, California
**Highest Annual
Average Rainfall:**
Henderson Lake, British
Columbia
**Lowest Annual Average
Rainfall:** Bataques, Mexico

Longest Glacier:
Bering Glacier, Alaska
(204 kilometres)
**Largest Piedmont
Glacier:** Malaspina Glacier,
Alaska (3,900 square
kilometres)

ALASKA & CANADA

Canada is the second largest country in the world. Stretching across two-fifths of the continent of North America, it covers six time zones. It is a country of great contrasts. There are vast wheat-growing prairies, lofty snow-capped mountains and dense forests. Canada is the world's largest exporter of forest products such as timber. The northern part of the country stretches into the icy Arctic Ocean. Most of the major cities are situated in the south, along the border with the United States. This border is the longest between any two countries. The Rocky Mountains lie towards the west. Alaska, the largest state in the United States, lies west of Canada. The Inuit (or Eskimo) people live in the far north of Canada and Alaska. Polar bears, walruses and humpback whales are found here.

NATURAL LANDMARK

Niagara Falls

Niagara Falls lies between Canada and the United States. The spectacular waterfall gets its name from the native American word, 'onguiaahra', which means 'the strait'. The Canadian Niagara Falls is also called Horseshoe Falls, as it is shaped like a horseshoe. It drops over 50 metres.

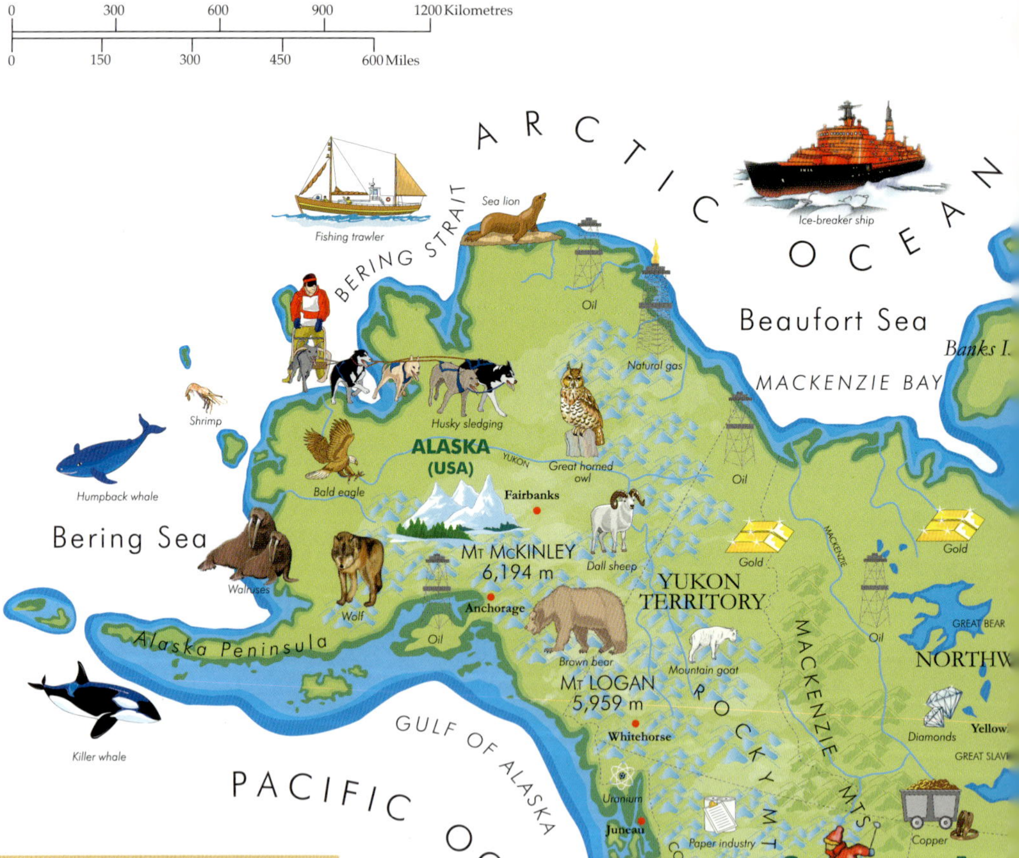

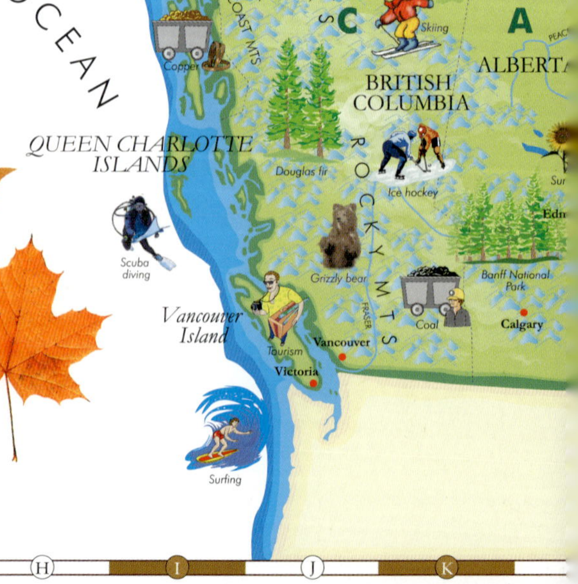

FLORA AND FAUNA

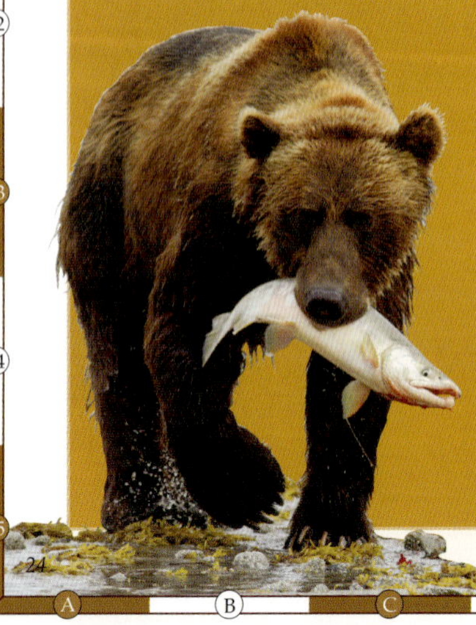

The Grizzly Bear is found on the steep slopes of the Canadian Rockies and parts of Alaska. This fierce hunter is the largest brown bear in the world. It is strong enough to carry a deer uphill.

Maple trees grow in large numbers in Canada. The sap of these trees is used to make maple syrup. Quebec, in eastern Canada, produces more maple syrup than any other place in the world.

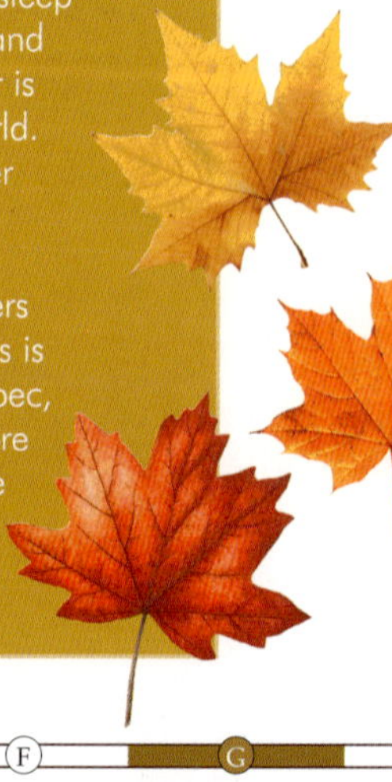

ARCTIC OCEAN

Fishing trawler

Sea lion

Ice-breaker ship

Beaufort Sea

Banks I.

MACKENZIE BAY

Oil

Husky sledging

Natural gas

Shrimp

Humpback whale

ALASKA (USA)

Great horned owl

Bald eagle

Fairbanks

YUKON

Oil

Gold

Gold

GREAT BEAR

Bering Sea

Mt McKINLEY 6,194 m

Dall sheep

YUKON TERRITORY

Oil

NORTHW

Walruses

Anchorage

Wolf

Brown bear

Mountain goat

Mt LOGAN 5,959 m

Diamonds

Yellow

GREAT SLAVE

Killer whale

Alaska Peninsula

Oil

GULF OF ALASKA

Whitehorse

PACIFIC OCEAN

Uranium

Juneau

Paper industry

Skiing

Copper

A

ALBERT

Copper

C

BRITISH COLUMBIA

QUEEN CHARLOTTE ISLANDS

Douglas fir

Ice hockey

Edm

Sur

Scuba diving

Grizzly bear

Banff National Park

Coal

Calgary

Vancouver Island

Tourism

Vancouver

Victoria

Surfing

| 0 | 300 | 600 | 900 | 1200 Kilometres |
| 0 | 150 | 300 | 450 | 600 Miles |

FESTIVALS AND FAIRS

The Calgary Stampede is a ten-day-long celebration that takes place every year in July, in Calgary, in the Canadian province of Alberta. The Stampede was first held in 1923, when Alberta became a centre for cattle trade. The festival is famous for its rodeo and bull-riding shows. Another attraction is the chuck-wagon race, in which horse-drawn wagons race to the finish line. Music shows are held in the city, and there are also free pancakes for breakfast for everyone!

FACT FILE

CANADA
Capital: Ottawa
Population: 38,005,238
Languages: English, French
Currency: Canadian dollar
Area: 9,976,140 square kilometres
Major Industries: Timber, paper production, diamond processing, iron industry, shipbuilding
Longest River: Mackenzie River (4,241 kilometres)
Highest Peak: Mt Logan (5,959 metres)

ALASKA
Capital: Juneau
Population: 736,081
Language: English
Currency: US dollar
Area: 1,530,700 sq km
Major Industries: Oil drilling, fishing, tourism
Longest River: Yukon River (3,190 km)
Highest Peak: Mt McKinley (6,190 metres)

GREENLAND (Denmark)

Bailey glacier
Ellesmere Island
QUEEN ELIZABETH ISLANDS
Oil
Traditional igloo
BAFFIN BAY
Polar bear
Arctic hare
Walruses
Narwhals
Baffin Island
Musk ox
Petroleum industry
Victoria Island
DAVIS STRAIT
Musk ox
Porpoise
Grizzly bear
Lead
Inuit (Eskimo)
HUDSON STRAIT
Labrador Sea
Arctic fox
ST TERRITORIES
Tourism
Wolf
Hooded seal
LABRADOR
NEWFOUNDLAND
Fishing industry
Beluga whales
Lacrosse
Moose
HUDSON BAY
Iron ore
Canada goose
Cycling
Tourism
St John's
LAKE ATHABASCA
Wheat
Cattle
NELSON
Timber
Bald eagle
Maple syrup
Viking settlement
Fishing industry
QUEBEC
Cape Breton Island
Oil
SASKATCHEWAN
Wheat
MANITOBA
LAKE WINNIPEG
ONTARIO
Pigs
Baseball
Prince Edward Island
Quebec
NEW BRUNSWICK
NOVA SCOTIA
Cargo ship
Royal Canadian Mountie
Cattle
Wheat
Copper
Gold
Fredericton
Halifax
Cycling
Uranium
Cattle
Regina
Winnipeg
Maple leaf leaves
Uranium
Bata Shoe museum
Pears
Montreal Olympic Stadium
Montreal
Ocean kayaking
Sunflowers
LAKE SUPERIOR
CN Tower
Ottawa
N A D A
Cherries
Toronto
LAKE HURON
ST LAWRENCE
ATLANTIC OCEAN
S A
Hamilton
Niagara Falls
Steel industry
LAKE ERIE

NORTH EASTERN STATES OF THE USA

The eastern coast of the United States is surrounded by the Atlantic Ocean. In the north, Maine's rocky shores give way to the harbours of Boston and New York. The first British settlers in America settled along the East Coast. Inland, the wooded Appalachian Mountains run north to south. The five great lakes - Superior, Michigan, Huron, Erie and Ontario are located in this region. New York, Chicago and Washington, the great cities of skyscrapers, are situated in this region. Many industries have developed around local iron and coal deposits. Aircraft, machinery and cars are exported. Oil, natural gas and hydroelectric power are used for energy. The farms in the northeast are smaller than those on the western plains. Cereals and vegetables are grown, and cattle, sheep, pigs and poultry are reared.

MAN-MADE LANDMARK

Statue of Liberty

The Statue of Liberty overlooks the New York harbour. Gifted by France in 1886, it is a symbol of political freedom and democracy. Sightseers can climb right to the top of this national monument.

FESTIVALS AND FAIRS

Independence Day - 4th July - celebrates the Declaration of Independence in 1776. The day is marked by colourful parades, patriotic speeches and fireworks.

FACT FILE

UNITED STATES OF AMERICA
Capital: Washington, DC
Area: 9,629,091 square kilometres
Population: 328,329,953
Languages: English, Spanish
Currency: US dollar
Major Industries: Petroleum, steel, motor vehicles, aerospace, telecommunications, chemicals, electronics, food processing, consumer goods, lumber, mining
Major Rivers: Arkansas, Colorado, Mississippi, Missouri, Rio Grande, Snake, Yukon
Major Peaks: McKinley, North Peak, Blackburn, Sanford, Bona

Fishing industry

Potatoes

Poultry

Iron ore

Cheese

Printing industry

Dairy

NORTH DAKOTA

MINNESOTA

Barley

Duluth

LAKE SUPERIOR

Fishing trawler

Iron ore

Timber

Copper

Deer

Tourism

MICHIGAN

LAKE ERIE

Carrots

Golf

WISCONSIN

Rye

Computer industry

St Paul

Sugar maple leaves

Snow mobile

Fishing industry

Canada goose

Minneapolis

Cheese

Apples

SOUTH DAKOTA

American football

Soya beans

Potatoes

Cranberries

LAKE MICHIGAN

Grand Rapids

Chemic

Deer

Corn

Tourism

Milwaukee

Lansing

Sioux City

Madison

Sears Towers

Chicago

Car industry

Detr

NEBRASKA

Pigs

Bald eagle

IOWA

Electronics

Car industry

Des Moines

Poultry

Lead

Corn

Hamburger

Paper industry

Tomatoes

INDIANA

Peaches

Grapes

ILLINOIS

Electronics

Sugar maple leaves

Basketball

Basel

Corn

Dairy

Indianapolis

Cincina

Car industry

Springfield

Coal

Sheep

Kansas City

Jefferson City

MISSOURI

St Louis

Gateway Arch

Oil

Wild turkey

Pigs

Louisville

Tobacco

Frankf

KANSAS

Jazz

Derby

Bourbon whis

Poultry

MISSOURI

Soya beans

Cotton

Natural gas

KENT

Springfield

Pine trees

TENNESSEE

FACT FILE

CONNECTICUT
Capital: Hartfort
Area: 12,548 square kilometres

DELAWARE
Capital: Dover
Area: 5,060 square kilometres

ILLINOIS
Capital: Springfield
Area: 143,962 square kilometres

INDIANA
Capital: Indianapolis
Area: 92,895 square kilometres

IOWA
Capital: Des Moines
Area: 144,700 square kilometres

KENTUCKY
Capital: Frankfort
Area: 102,895 square kilometres

MAINE
Capital: Augusta
Area: 79,932 square kilometres

MARYLAND
Capital: Annapolis
Area: 25,314 square kilometres

MASSACHUSETTS
Capital: Boston
Area: 20,305 square kilometres

MICHIGAN
Capital: Lansing
Area: 147,122 square kilometres

MINNESOTA
Capital: St Paul
Area: 206,189 square kilometres

MISSOURI
Capital: Jefferson City
Area: 178,414 square kilometres

NEW HAMPSHIRE
Capital: Concord
Area: 23,227 square kilometres

NEW JERSEY
Capital: Trenton
Area: 19,210 square kilometres

NEW YORK
Capital: Albany
Area: 122,284 square kilometres

OHIO
Capital: Columbus
Area: 106,055 square kilometres

PENNSYLVANIA
Capital: Harrisburg
Area: 116,075 square kilometres

RHODE ISLANDS
Capital: Providence
Area: 2,706 square kilometres

VERMONT
Capital: Montpelier
Area: 23,957 square kilometres

WEST VIRGINIA
Capital: Charleston
Area: 62,362 square kilometres

WISCONSIN
Capital: Madison
Area: 140,662 square kilometres

Scale:
0 100 200 300 400 500 Kilometres
0 50 100 150 200 250 300 Miles

CANADA

Moose
Potatoes
Pine trees
MAINE
Timber
Shrimp
Poultry
Augusta
Sugar maple syrup
Seals
Textile industry
VERMONT
Montpelier
NEW HAMPSHIRE
Printing industry
Concord
Tourism
Harvard University
Boston
St Lawrence
LAKE ONTARIO
NEW YORK
Natural gas
Albany
MASSACHUSETTS
Ladybug
Providence
Dairy
Hartford
RHODE ISLAND
CONNECTICUT
Cargo ship
LAKE ERIE
Niagara Falls
Brown bear
APPALACHIAN MTS
Statue of Liberty
Fish
Fish
Chocolates
Skiing
New York
Industry
Steel industry
Cattle
Wild turkey
Cleveland
Trenton
NEW JERSEY
PENNSYLVANIA
Harrisburg
Philadelphia
Akron
Soya beans
Pittsburgh
Coal
Natural gas
Baltimore
Chemical industry
Yachting
OHIO
Coal
Dover
Columbus
Textile industry
White House
Washington DC
DELAWARE
WEST VIRGINIA
WASHINGTON
MARYLAND
Cheese
Livestock
Ohio
Charleston
Skiing
Richmond
Coal
Cherries
VIRGINIA
Cattle
CKY
Tobacco
Peanuts
Woodpecker
Fishing trawler
ATLANTIC OCEAN
Crabs
N
NORTH CAROLINA

FLORA AND FAUNA

The Mayflower is the official flower of the state of Massachusetts. The waxy pink or white flowers with oval, hairy leaves were christened by the first settlers after their ship, the 'Mayflower'. When the ship reached the American shores in Plymouth, these flowers were in bloom.

In 1782, the Bald Eagle was chosen as the emblem of the United States because of its majestic looks. This powerful bird is now endangered due to poisoning by pesticides. Efforts are being made to increase its population.

WESTERN STATES OF THE USA

The western coast of the United States is lapped by the Pacific Ocean. The steep rocky mountains with their jagged peaks run from Canada down to Mexico. Many rivers start in the Rockies, and some have cut deep valleys and canyons. The western slopes of these mountains catch the rain from the Pacific. The eastern slopes and the Great Plains beyond them are dry. The conifer-forested states of Oregon and Washington are cool and wet. Further south, San Francisco and Los Angles are sunny and warm. California is known for its fruits, like peaches, oranges and grapes. Winemaking is a big industry here. The Silicon Valley, known for its high-tech computer industry, is also in California.

MAN-MADE LANDMARK
Mt Rushmore

The world's greatest mountain carving has been sculptured out of the rock face of Mt Rushmore, in the Black Hills of South Dakota. This epic sculpture, made between 1921 and 1947, features the faces of four American presidents - George Washington, Thomas Jefferson, Theodore Roosevelt and Abraham Lincoln.

HAWAIIAN ISLANDS (USA)

Niihau · Kauai · Oahu · Honolulu · Tourism · Molokai · Lanai · Maui · Sugar cane · Kahoolawe · Pineapples · HAWAII · Coral reefs · Kilauea Volcano

PACIFIC OCEAN

Douglas firs · Hamburger · Golden Gate · San Francisco · Computer industry

FESTIVALS AND FAIRS

Halloween, on October 31, is an occasion to dress up and have fun. The origin of Halloween goes back to early times when it was celebrated as a festival of fire. People believed that spirits of the dead roamed about on that day.

FACT FILE

ARIZONA
Capital: Phoenix
Area: 294,313 square kilometres

CALIFORNIA
Capital: Sacramento
Area: 403,932 square kilometres

HAWAII
Capital: Honolulu
Area: 16,635 square kilometres

IDAHO
Capital: Boise
Area: 214,314 square kilometres

KANSAS
Capital: Topeka
Area: 211,900 square kilometres

MONTANA
Capital: Helena
Area: 376,978 square kilometres

NEBRASKA
Capital: Lincoln
Area: 199,098 square kilometres

NEVADA
Capital: Carson City
Area: 284,448 square kilometres

NEW MEXICO
Capital: Santa Fe
Area: 314,311 square kilometres

NORTH DAKOTA
Capital: Bismarck
Area: 178,647 square kilometres

OKLAHOMA
Capital: Oklahoma City
Area: 177,847 square kilometres

OREGON
Capital: Salem
Area: 248,631 square kilometres

SOUTH DAKOTA
Capital: Pierre
Area: 196,541 square kilometres

UTAH
Capital: Salt Lake City
Area: 212,752 square kilometres

WASHINGTON
Capital: Olympia
Area: 172,348 square kilometres

WYOMING
Capital: Cheyenne
Area: 251,488 square kilometres

FLORA AND FAUNA

The coniferous redwood tree, also known as the Sequoia tree, is California's state tree. It is the tallest tree in the world, with many reaching over 107 metres tall. The diameter of the tree can be about 5 metres. California has many coastal redwood forests.

Found in the Rockies and other parts of America, the cougar, or the mountain lion, belongs to the cat family. It is lithe and agile, and eats a varied menu, from deer to rabbits and birds. The Incas of Peru called it the Puma.

CANADA

WASHINGTON
Seattle
Olympia
Aircraft industry
Wheat
Copper
Silver
Columbia
Spokane
Dam
Lead
Sheep
Great Falls
Timber
Portland
Cherries
Peas
Skiing
Wine
CASCADE RANGE
Salem
Pears
Dairy
IDAHO
Natural gas
MONTANA
Helena
Wheat
Cattle
Petroleum industry
Sugar beet
Oil
MISSOURI
Sunflowers
Buffalo
Wheat
Grand Forks
NORTH DAKOTA
Bismarck
Fargo
Dairy
MINNESOTA

OREGON
Wheat
Paper industry
Boise
Computer industry
Elk
Idaho Falls
Skiing
Tourism
Rodeo
Cool
Barley
Wheat
SOUTH DAKOTA
Gold
Pierre
Corn
ROCKY MTS
Timber
Sugar beet
Potatoes
Wheat
Bison
WYOMING MTS
Uranium
Mt Rushmore
Pine trees
Sunflowers
IOWA

Wild turkey
Honey bee
Sheep
Computer industry
Gold
Salt Lake City
Steel industry
Cattle
Petroleum industry
Cheyenne
Dinosaur fossils
Canada goose
NEBRASKA
Deer
Dairy
CALIFORNIA
SIERRA NEVADA
Reno
Silver
GREAT BASIN
Oil
UTAH
Gold
Copper
Denver
Tourism
Corn
Potatoes
Sunflowers
Strawberries
Lincoln
Carson City
Gold
Mt Elbert 4,339 m
Wheat
Corn
Wheat
Cattle
MISSOURI

NEVADA
Tourism
American Indian
Elk
COLORADO
Electronics
Baseball
Natural gas
Wigwam
KANSAS
Wichita
Kansas City
Oranges
Rodeo
Honey bee
Copper
Coal
Timber
Uranium
Steel industry
Wheat
Car industry
Tulsa
Petroleum industry
MOJAVE DESERT
Vineyards
Dairy
Casino
Las Vegas
Rodeo
Sheep
Computer industry
Santa Fe
Livestock
Oklahoma City
ARKANSAS
Strawberries
Getty Centre
Los Angeles
Gold
Rattle snake
Citrus fruits
Golf
Potatoes
Albuquerque
Beer
OKLAHOMA
Violin
Wild turkey
San Diego
Aircraft industry
ARIZONA
Phoenix
Aircraft industry
NEW MEXICO
Tourism
Onions
Wine
Bison
Cotton
Cactus
Gold
Chillis
Petroleum industry
Copper
Tucson
Vineyards
El Paso

MEXICO

TEXAS

0 150 300 450 600 Kilometres
0 75 150 225 300 Miles

SOUTHERN STATES OF THE USA

The southern states have a hot climate. The huge state of Texas is famous for cattle ranching. Business centres like Houston and Dallas are located here. The northeastern parts of this region have huge wheatfields, and the soil is rich. The entire area is known for its tornadoes. Several large rivers meander across the plains. The Mississippi-Missouri river system is the fourth longest in the world. It flows into the Gulf of Mexico. The gulf is fringed by swamps and creeks, where alligators, ibis and pelicans live. This part has a humid climate. The southern part of Florida has swampy wetlands known as the Everglades. Cotton, rice, sugarcane and tobacco do well in this warm and well-watered land. Sometimes these areas get flooded after heavy rain.

Map labels

KANSAS

NEW MEXICO

OKLAHOMA

ARKANSAS

Natural gas

Wheat

Amarillo

Cotton

Armadillo

Owl

Lubbock

Sheep

Prairie dog

Computer industry

The Sixth Floor Museum

Dallas

Fort Worth

Aircraft industry

American football

Pine trees

Little Rock

Diamonds

Oil

LOUISIANA

Steer

Sweet potato

Shreveport

El Paso

RIO GRANDE

Cactus

Chilli pepper

Pecan nut

Petroleum refinery

Tourism

T E X A S

Timber

Baseball

Monarch butterflies

PECOS

Oil

Dairy

Iron ore

Waco

BRAZOS

Cattle

Rice

Cotton

The Alamo

Austin

COLORADO

Houston Astrodome

Houston

Pelican

Oil

San Antonio

Whooping crane

Fishing industry

Oil

Rattle snake

MEXICO

Tomatoes

Corpus Christi

RIO GRANDE

Citrus fruits

Shrimp

Oil rig

Crabs

N

0   100   200   300   400   500 Kilometres

0   50   100   150   200   250   300 Miles

FLORA AND FAUNA

The Pecan is the tree of Texas. This large tree bears long, pointed nuts with a shell. Pecan nuts are tasty and often used in chocolates, cakes and desserts.

Alligators can be found in the coastal swamps of Carolina, along the tip of Florida and in the coastal parts of the Gulf of Mexico. These large, scaly reptiles with powerful jaws feed on fish, mammals, turtles and birds. Because American alligators were becoming rare, they are now protected by various laws.

INDIANA
ILLINOIS
OURI
KENTUCKY
WEST VIRGINIA
VIRGINIA

Violin
Jazz music
Memphis
Piano
Bald eagle
Corn
Dairy
MISSISSIPPI
Electronics
Jackson
ane
Ducks
Soya beans
Baton Rouge
Oil
Jazz music
New Orleans
Tourism
Killer whales

Footwear industry
Nashville
Dairy
TENNESSEE
Chattanooga
Wild turkey
TENNESSEE
Birmingham
ALABAMA
Textile industry
Montgomery
Poultry
ALABAMA
Dairy
Timber
Cotton
Peanuts
Oil
Mobile
Peanuts
Shrimp
Space camp
Car industry
Columbus
Citrus fruits
Cotton
Pecan nut

APPALACHIN MTS
Knoxville
Timber
Greensboro
Raleigh
Poultry
Electronics
Pigs
Textile industry
Peanuts
NORTH CAROLINA
Charlotte
Cococola industry
Atlanta
GEORGIA
Peaches
Timber
SOUTH CAROLINA
Columbia
Tobacco
Timber
Charleston
SAVANNAH
Tobacco
Savannah
Alligator
Tourism
Fish
Cargo ship

ATLANTIC OCEAN

Shrimp
Cargo ship
Dolphins

Tallahassee
Livestock
Jacksonville
Timber
Shrimp
UNIVERSAL
Universal Studios Theme Park
Orlando
Walt Disney World Resort
Cape of canaveral
Tampa
FLORIDA
Citrus fruits
Aircraft industry
Alligator
Fort Lauderdale
Windsurfing
Miami
Tourism
Sailing
Fish

GULF OF MEXICO

FACT FILE

ALABAMA
Capital: Montgomery
Area: 131,426 square kilometres

ARKANSAS
Capital: Little Rock
Area: 134,856 square kilometres

FLORIDA
Capital: Tallahassee
Area: 139,670 square kilometres

GEORGIA
Capital: Atlanta
Area: 149,976 square kilometres

LOUISIANA
Capita: Baton Rouge
Area: 112,825 square kilometres

MISSISSIPPI
Capital: Jackson
Area: 121,489 square kilometres

NORTH CAROLINA
Capital: Raleigh
Area: 126,161 square kilometres

SOUTH CAROLINA
Capital: Columbia
Area: 77,982 square kilometres

TENNESSEE
Capital: Nashville
Area: 106,752 square kilometres

TEXAS
Capital: Austin
Area: 678,051 square kilometres

FESTIVALS AND FAIRS

The hundred-year-old Texas State Fair is held for a month, every fall, in Fair Park. Apart from the thrilling bronco busting rodeo, America's biggest ferris wheel, the Texas Star, is located here.

MAN-MADE LANDMARK

The John F. Kennedy Space Center at Cape Canaveral in Florida is the only space shuttle launch complex in the United States. When a rocket-powered shuttle blasts off into space, there is a powerful boom and clouds of smoke and vapour.

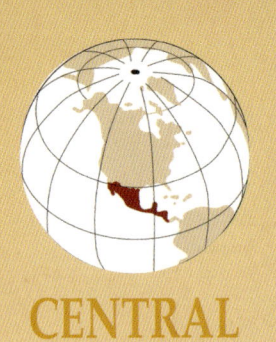

CENTRAL AMERICA

Central America is a wedge-shaped neck of land that links North America to South America. To the north lies Mexico with its varied landscape of vast deserts, snow-capped mountains and tropical rainforests. To the south of Mexico are seven countries of Central America. This region has mountains and volcanoes. Now and then the volcanoes erupt. Hurricanes strike the coastal areas often. To the east a string of islands, often called the West Indies, stretch out over the Caribbean Sea. Rainforests cover much of Central America. Jaguars, tapirs, capuchin and howler monkeys and toucans are found here. Tourists come to see the ruins of the Mayan and Aztec civilizations, and enjoy the white coral sand beaches. Sugar canes, bananas and other crops grow here. In the south, the Panama Canal, a waterway for ships, connects the Atlantic and the Pacific oceans.

MAN-MADE LANDMARK

El Castillo, a pyramid built in nine terraces, is actually the Mayan calendar, made in stone. It lies in the ruins of Chichen Itza, an ancient Mayan city built in the sixth century, in the Yucatan Peninsula.

FESTIVALS AND FAIRS

Junkanoo, the national festival of the Bahamas, is celebrated on two days - December 26 and January 1. It is celebrated with parades, intricate costumes and music.

FACT FILE

 **ANTIGUA & BARBUDA** **Capital:** Saint John's

 **REPUBLIC OF COSTA RICA** **Capital:** San Jose

 **REPUBLIC OF CUBA** **Capital:** Havana

 **REPUBLIC OF EL SALVADOR** **Capital:** San Salvador.

 **ARUBA** **Capital:** Oranjestad

 **GRENADA** **Capital:** Saint George's

 **COMMONWEALTH OF DOMINICA** **Capital:** Roseau

 DEPARTMENT OF GUADELOUPE **Capital:** Basse-Terre

 COMMONWEALTH OF THE BAHAMAS **Capital:** Nassau

 BELIZE **Capital:** Belmopan

 **DOMINICAN REPUBLIC** **Capital:** Santo Domingo

 **REPUBLIC OF GAUTEMALA** **Capital:** Guatemala City

 BARBADOS **Capital:** Bridgetown

N

USA

ATLANTIC OCEAN

FLORA AND FAUNA

Found in the Sonoran Desert in northwestern Mexico, the saguaro cactus is the tallest of all desert plants. The saguaro can grow to 12 metres in height and live for over 200 years. When it sops up one summer rainfall, it can expand its girth by 50 per cent.

The Central American scarlet macaw is found in Mexico, Guatemala and Belize. This red-and-yellow bird has white patches on the face and touches of blue or green on the wings. It eats fruits, nuts, flowers and nectar.

Fishing trawler

GULF OF MEXICO

STRAITS OF FLORIDA

FLORIDA

BAHAMAS
Nassau

Snorkelling
Tourism
Turtle
Coral reefs
Cruise liner
Coral reefs

Havana
Sugar cane
CUBA
Cigars
Citrus fruits

DOMINICAN REPUBLIC
Goat
HAITI
Gold
Santo Domingo
Port-Au-Prince

Tobacco
San Juan
PUERTO RICO (USA)

ANTIGUA & BARBUDA
ST KITTS & NEVIS
GUADELOUPE (FR.)
DOMINICA

ST LUCIA

ST VINCENT & THE GRENADINES
BARBADOS
Tourism

GRENADA

TRINIDAD & TOBAGO
Boa constrictor

Lobsters
Fish

Merida (city)
Cattle
Yucatan Peninsula
Oil
Coffee
Coral reefs

Turtle
GAYMAN ISLANDS

Sugar cane
Kingston
Reggae guitar
JAMAICA

Sharks

Sailing

Snorkelling

Fish

BELIZE
Tikal
Belmopan

GUATEMALA **HONDURAS**
Bananas
Coffee
Guatemala City
Bananas
Coffee
Tegucigalpa
Bananas
Fishing industry

NICARAGUA
San Salvador
Coffee
EL SALVADOR
Managua
Cotton
Coffee

San Jose
Balu volcano
COSTA RICA
PANAMA
Bananas

Caribbean Sea

Aruba (Neth)
Netherlands Antilles

Panama canal
Panama City
Timber

COLOMBIA

VENEZUELA

0	200	400	600	800	1000 Kilometres
0	100 200	300	400	500	600 Miles

REPUBLIC OF HAITI
Capital: Port-au-Prince

REPUBLIC OF HONDURAS
Capital: Tegucigalpa

JAMAICA
Capital: Kingston

NETHERLANDS ANTILLES
Capital: Willemstad

UNITED MEXICAN STATES
Capital: Mexico City

REPUBLIC OF NICARAGUA
Capital: Managua

DEPARTMENT OF MARTINIQUE
Capital: Fort-de-France

REPUBLIC OF PANAMA
Capital: Panama

COMMONWEALTH OF PUERTO RICO
Capital: San Juan

FEDERATION OF SAINT KITTS & NEVIS
Capital: Basseterre

SAINT LUCIA
Capital: Castries

SAINT VINCENT & THE GRENADINES
Capital: Kingstown

REPUBLIC OF TRINIDAD & TOBAGO
Capital: Port-of-Spain

SOUTH AMERICA

South America is the world's fourth largest continent. In the northwest, the Isthmus of Panama links it to North America. Drake Passage, south of Cape Horn, separates the continent from Antarctica. The Amazon, the second longest river at 6,436 kilometres, flows across Brazil. It contains about 20 per cent of the world's freshwater. Huge tropical rainforests grow in the Amazon Basin. These forests contain more plants than any other place in the world. More than 2,500 types of trees, hundreds of kinds of orchids and unique wildlife are found here. Although rainforests have been greatly harmed by human activities, steps are being taken to stop the damage. The world's longest range of mountains, the Andes, stretch from Colombia to Chile, along the Pacific coast. Mt Aconcagua lies along the border of Argentina and Chile. In Argentina and Paraguay, there are vast grasslands called the pampas where gauchos (cowboys) raise beef cattle.

Over half the population of South America live in Brazil. Most major cities lie along the coast, or on large rivers. The continent is rich in iron ore, copper, tin and oil reserves. The emeralds of Colombia are well known. Rubber, cocoa, coffee, quinine, sisal, sugar, wheat and wool are produced here. In the 1400s, the Inca civilization flourished in the Andes. In the 1500s, settlers from Spain and Portugal came in search of gold and silver. Many intermarried with the local people and produced a mixed race known as mestizos.

Easter Island Statues

GULF OF MEXICO

CENTRAL AMERICA

GULF OF PANAMA

GALAPAGOS ISLANDS

PACIFIC OCEAN

TROPIC OF CAPRICORN

JUAN FERNANDEZ ISLANDS

VENEZUELA
COLOMBIA
GUYANA
SURINAME
FRENCH GUIANA
ATLANTIC OCEAN
ECUADOR
PERU
BRAZIL
BOLIVIA
PARAGUAY
PACIFIC OCEAN
CHILE
ARGENTINA
URUGUAY
ATLANTIC OCEAN
FALKLAND ISLANDS (UK)

0   600   1200 Kilometres
0   400   800 Miles

N

Caribbean Sea

Lesser Antilles

ATLANTIC OCEAN

LAKE MARACAIBO

ORINOCO

GUIANA HIGHLANDS

META

BLANCO

NEGRO

AMAZON Fan

JAPURA

NAPO

PUTUMAYO

A M A Z O N
B A S I N

AMAZON

TOCANTINS

JURUA

PURUS

MADEIRA

TAPAJÓS

XINGU

ARAGUAIA

PARNAIBA

SÃO FRANCISCO

PLATEAU OF
BORBOREMA

MADRE DE DIOS

GUAPORE

MAMORE

PLATEAU OF
MATO GROSSO

BRAZILIAN HIGHLANDS

A
N
D
E
S

ATACAMA DESERT

GRAN CHACO

PARAGUAY

PARANÁ

SERRA DA MANTIQUERA

SERRA DO MAR

IGUACU FALLS

URUGUAY

SALADO

PARANA

TROPIC OF CAPRICORN

MESOPOTAMIA

ATLANTIC OCEAN

▲ MT ACONCAGUA
6,960 m

PAMPAS

Rio de la plata

COLORADO

NEGRO

Bahia Blanca

CHUBUT

GULF
OF
SAN MATIAS

PATAGONIA

0	500	1000	1500	2000 Kilometres
0	250	500	750	1000 Miles

FALKLAND ISLANDS

TIERRA DEL FUEGO

CAPE HORN

FACT FILE

Longest River: Amazon
Highest Peak: Aconcagua
(6,959 metres)
Largest Desert: Patagonian,
Argentina
Active Volcano: Santa Maria,
Guatemala
Largest Lake: Maracaibo
(13,280 square kilometres)
Lowest Point: Salinas Grandes
Valdés Peninsula
**Highest Recorded
Temperature:**
120° F, in Rivadavia, Argentina
**Lowest Recorded
Temperature:**
-27° F, in Sarmiento, Argentina
**Highest Annual Average
Rainfall:** Quibdo, Colombia
**Lowest Annual Average
Rainfall:** Arica, Chile
Highest Waterfall: Angel Fall
(979 metres)

Highest Lake: Lake Titicaca,
Peru
(3,810 metres above sea level)
Longest Mountain Range:
Andes

World Heritage site:
Maya Site of Copan

NORTHERN SOUTH AMERICA

The Amazon, the second longest river in the world, crosses Brazil. Here grows the largest rainforest in the world, with an enormous variety of plants and wildlife. To the west lie the Andes Mountains which stretch through Colombia, Ecuador, Peru, Bolivia and southwards. Further north, River Orinoco flows through Venezuela. Jaguars, sloths and toucans are found in the tropical forest around the basin. Native Indians still live in the forests. They hunt fish and gather plants for food and medicine, like quinine for malaria. The Amazon rainforest is being felled by loggers at an alarming rate. To the north of Brazil are the rugged Guiana Highlands. Colombia is the largest producer of natural emeralds in the world. Oil is found in Venezuela, Ecuador and Peru. Brazil is rich in minerals. Maize, sugarcane, bananas, coffee, cocoa, rubber and potatoes are all grown in this region.

ATLANTIC OCEAN

PACIFIC OCEAN

VENEZUELA

COLOMBIA

ECUADOR

PERU

BOLIVIA

GUYANA

SURI...

BRAZIL

PARAGUAY

...GENTINA

Barranquilla
Cartagena
Sheep
Medellin
Coal
Manizales
Bogota
Cali
Coffee
Oil
Quito
Llama
Orchids
Deer
Shrimp
Fishing industry
Mt COTOPAXI 5,896 m
Coffee
Iquitos
Timber
Toucan
Humming bird
Rubber tree
Jaguar
Piura
Petroleum refinery
Chiclayo
Llama
Trujillo
Sheep
Copper
Fishing trawler
Lima
Fishing industry
Sea lion
Pigs
Arequipa
Dolphins
La Paz
Potatoes
Coffee
Machu Picchu
Skiing
Cochabamba
Sucre
Santa Cruz
Copper
Natural gas
Caracas
Valencia
Oil
Barquisimeto
Ciudad Bolivar
Anaconda
Giant otter
Georgetown
Gold
Angel Falls
Bananas
Citrus fruits
Oil
AMAZON BASIN
Teatro Amazonas
Manaus
Anaconda
Cattle
Citrus fruits
Porto Velho
Iguana
Gold
Rubber tree
Sloth
Wolf
Cuiaba
Sheep
Puma
Textile industry
LAKE MARACAIBO
Oil
Petrochemical industry
Sugar cane
Turtle
Fish
Oil
NEGRO
ORINOCO
PURUS
MADERA
PARANA

| 0 | 300 | 600 | 900 | 1200 Kilometres |
| 0 | 150 | 300 | 450 | 600 | 750 Miles |

FACT FILE

REPUBLIC OF BOLIVIA
Capital: La Paz
Area: 1,098,580 square kilometres

REPUBLIC OF ECUADOR
Capital: Quito
Area: 283,560 square kilometres

REPUBLIC OF PERU
Capital: Lima
Area: 1,285,220 square kilometres

FEDERATIVE REPUBLIC OF BRAZIL
Capital: Brasilia
Area: 8,511,965 square kilometres

FRENCH GUIANA
Capital: Cayenne
Area: 91,000 square kilometres

REPUBLIC OF SURINAME
Capital: Paramaribo
Area: 163,270 square kilometres

REPUBLIC OF COLOMBIA
Capital: Bogota
Area: 1,138,910 square kilometres

CO-OPERATIVE REPUBLIC OF GUYANA
Capital: Georgetown
Area: 214,970 square kilometres

REPUBLIC OF VENEZUELA
Capital: Caracas
Area: 912,050 square kilometres

FLORA AND FAUNA

Brazil is the largest coffee producer in the world. The coffee plant is a small shrub with white flowers and red berries. The berries are skinned to take out the coffee beans. These are then roasted and ground.

Llamas live in the Andes. They are used to carry goods to remote areas. They are reared for meat and hides. Their wool is spun into woollen cloth and ropes. Llamas are herbivores and can travel long distances without water.

FRENCH GUIANA
NAM
Cayenne
Jaguar
Fishing industry
Livestock
Belem
Piranha fish
Bananas
Windsurfing
Dolphins
Mangoes
Oranges
Fortaleza
Teresina
Palm trees
Natal
Coral reefs
Sugar cane
Cassava
Rice
Soya beans
Gold
Diamonds
Corn
Recife
Monkey
Boa constrictor
Cattle
Chemical industry
SAO FRANCISCO
Anteater
Cotton
Tourism
Nuts
Salvador
Cargo ship
Sugar cane
Hang gliding
Brasilia
Football
MATO GROSSO
Iron ore
Fish
Jaguar
Campo Grande
Belo Horizonte
Tobacco
Steel industry
Carnival
Campinas
Textile industry
Coffee
Rio de Janeiro
Oranges
Sao Paulo
Curitiba
Alligator
Fish
Cattle
Porto Alegre
Cargo ship

N

GALAPAGOS ISLANDS (ECUADOR)
Iguana
Isabela Island
Tourism

TICO OCEAN

MAN-MADE LANDMARK

Machu Pichu, the ruins of an ancient city of the Incas, were discovered in 1911, in the densely-forested Peruvian Andes. About 500 years ago, the Incas built palaces, temples, carved terraces and storehouses. More than 100 flights of steps link different levels of the site.

FESTIVALS AND FAIRS

In Rio de Janeiro, the Rio Carnival lasts for five days each year, before Lent. Thousands of Samba dancers, singers and drummers in elaborate costumes parade through the city in spectacular floats.

37

NATURAL LANDMARK

The river Iguassu ('great water') was so called by the Guarani Indians. It cascades over the borders of Argentina and Brazil. The spectacular falls are approximately 3 kilometres wide and are made up of over 275 separate waterfalls. Often, one can see rainbows peering through the curtain of mist.

SOUTHERN SOUTH AMERICA

The rugged Andes mountains run southward, dividing Chile and Argentina. Chile is a long, narrow country. In northern Chile lies the dry, barren Atacama Desert, where in parts it has not rained in living memory. Lush coastal forests, vineyards and orchards lie in the central valley, south of the desert. Paraguay, with its hot and humid climate, lies in the centre of the continent. To the west of Paraguay are the dry grasslands of the Grand Chaco; to the east are forests and fertile grasslands. Towards the Atlantic lies Uruguay. Argentina is a big country with vast fertile grasslands called the pampas, where cattle are reared for beef and hide. The famous cowboys, called gauchos, live here. Further south is the dry, windswept plateau of Patagonia. In this cold semi-desert sheep farmers graze their sheep on the thin grasses. Tourism is important here. People come to watch seabirds, penguins and seals.

A T L A N T I C
O C E A N

N

CAPE HORN

Sea lion
Comodoro Rivadavia
Oil
Sheep
Armadillo
Potatoes
Rio Gallegos
Moreno Glacier
Sheep
Punta Arenas
Oil
Mapuche Indian
King penguins
TIERRA DEL FUEGO
Toucan
Ushuaia
Fish
Fur seals

1600 Kilometres
1000 Miles
1200 — 750
800 — 500
400 — 250
0 — 0

FESTIVALS AND FAIRS

The festival of La Tirana is celebrated on July 16, in a village of the same name, near the Atacama Desert in Chile. Thousands of Chileans, mostly members of music and dance clubs, pay tribute to the Virgin Mary. They dance wearing traditional costumes and masks.

FLORA AND FAUNA

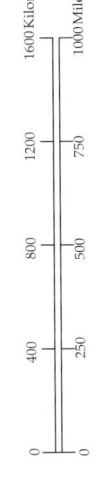

Grapes, grown in the summer in the Central Valley of Chile, are used to make wine. Vines were first brought to Chile by the Spanish.

The strange-looking anteater is found in Paraguay and Argentina. It has a long tongue and an extended snout, which is used like a vacuum cleaner to suck up ants and termites. It has short legs and a bushy tail and sharp claws for digging. The coat is grey with black and white markings.

FACT FILE

ARGENTINA

Capital: Buenos Aires
Population: 45,376,763
Languages: Spanish, English, Italian, German, French
Currency: Argentine peso
Area: 2,766,890 square kilometres
Major Industries: Food processing, motor vehicles, consumer durables, textiles, chemicals and petrochemicals, printing

REPUBLIC OF CHILE

Capital: Santiago
Population: 19,116,209
Language: Spanish
Currency: Chilean peso
Area: 756,950 square kilometres
Major Industries: Copper, foodstuffs, fish processing, iron and steel, wood and wood products, transport equipment, cement, textiles, wine

FALKLAND ISLANDS (ISLAS MALVINAS)

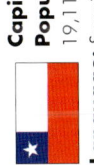

Capital: Port Stanley
Population: 3,354
Language: English
Currency: Falkland pound
Area: 12,173 square kilometres
Major Industries: Wool and fish processing, sale of stamps and coins, tourism

REPUBLIC OF PARAGUAY

Capital: Asuncion
Population: 7,132,530
Languages: Spanish, Guarani
Currency: Guarani
Area: 406,750 square kilometres
Major Industries: Sugar, cement, textiles, beverages, wood products, soybeans

ORIENTAL REPUBLIC OF URUGUAY

Capital: Montevideo
Population: 3,473,727
Languages: Spanish, Portunol, or Brazilero
Currency: Uruguayan Peso
Area: 176,220 square kilometres
Major Industries: Food processing, transportation equipment, petroleum products, textiles, chemicals, beverages

EUROPE

Europe is the second smallest continent in the world. In the far north lie the frozen Arctic islands of Svalbard. Reindeer and polar bears live here. The mountains of Scandinavia are the highest in the region. In the north Atlantic Ocean lies the island of Iceland, also known as the Land of Ice and Fire because of its volcanoes, geysers, icefields and glaciers. Extending eastward are Finland and the Baltic states of Estonia, Latvia and Lithuania, which are a part of the North European Plains. Some thickly-populated areas like the southern United Kingdom, northern France and Germany are also a part of this plain. The plain is Europe's most densely populated area. Northern Europe has a long, cold winter and a shorter summer. Fruits, vegetables, potatoes, wheat, oats and rye are grown here. The Arctic Ocean borders the north of the continent, while the Atlantic Ocean touches the western

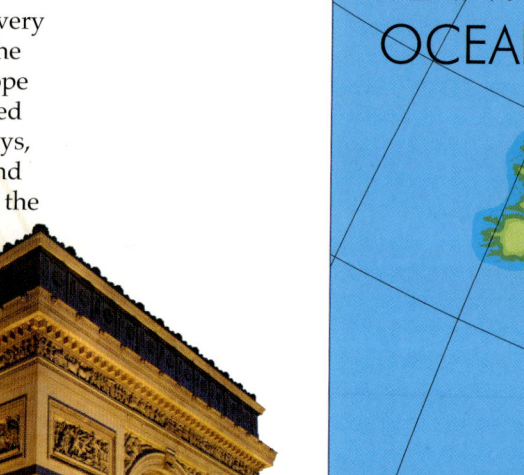

Euro Tunnel

countries. The Mediterranean Sea borders the southern part of Europe. Italy, Spain and Greece lie in the Mediterranean region. These countries enjoy sunny summers and mild winters. Citrus fruits and olives grow well in these parts.

Trading is very important to the economy. Europe is well connected by roads, railways, airports, canals and ports. A majority of the population lives in the cities and towns, working in factories and industries such as finance and tourism. The European Union is a group of 15 western European countries, which work and trade together. The union has a parliament as well as a court of justice.

Arc de Triomphe in Paris

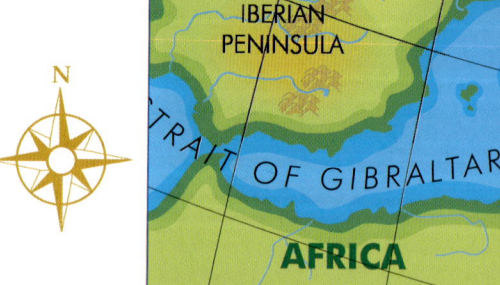

FACT FILE

Continent Size:
9,938,000 square kilometres
Longest River: Volga River
Largest Lake:
Ladoga, Russia
(17,678 square kilometres)
Active Volcano:
Mount Etna, Sicily
Highest Peak:
Mount Elbrus (5,633 metres)

KOLA PENINSULA

Norwegian Sea

White Sea

KJOLEN MTS

INARI

TORNE

MEZEN

PECHORA

PECHORA

OB

ASIA

GULF OF BOTHNIA

Lake Onega

DVINA

ONEGA

Lake Ladoga

URAL MTS

GULF OF FINLAND

Lake Chudskoye

KAMA

North Sea

Gotland

Baltic Sea

NIEMEN

CENTRAL RUSSIAN UPLANDS

VOLGA

VOLGA PLAINS

NORTH EUROPEAN PLAIN

VISTULA

WESER

RHINE

ELBE

ODER

DON

VOLGA

SEINE

MEUSE

NNEL

JURA

DANUBE

DNIESTER

BUG

DNIEPER

DON

Caspian Sea

MASSIF CENTRAL

RHONE

ALPS

PLAINS OF HUNGARY

CARPATHIANS

DANUBE

Sea of Azov

KUBAN

TEREK

MT ELBRUS 5,642 m

CAUCASUS MTS

KURA

Crimea Island

Black Sea

APENNINES

Adriatic Sea

Sardinia

ANATOLIA PLEATEAU

ARABIAN PENINSULA

TIGRIS

Sicily

Crete

Cyprus

Mediterranean Sea

0 250 500 750 1000 1250 Kilometres
0 150 300 450 600 750 Miles

Lowest Point:
Caspian Sea shore
Highest Recorded Temperature:
119.8° F, in Sicily, Italy
Lowest Recorded Temperature:
-72° F, in Ust'-Shchugor, Russia
Highest Annual Average Rainfall: Crkvice, Yugoslavia (now Montenegro)

Lowest Annual Average Rainfall: Montenegro
Deepest Lake:
Lake Baikal, Siberia
Longest Mountain Range: Alps
World Heritage site:
Banks of the Seine, Paris

The river Seine

FLORA AND FAUNA

Scots pines are the only native British pines. These large ever-green trees grow in the Scottish Highlands, as well as the Irish countryside. Ash, oak and willow trees also grow well in the British Isles.

Red deer are the largest land mammals in the British Isles. Male red deer have big horns, called antlers. The antlers may have up to 14 branches! These deer are mainly found in Scotland. They live in groups called herds.

MAN-MADE LANDMARK

Stonehenge, in Wiltshire, is about 4,000 years old. It consists of rings of huge stones. It is believed that ancient people used the shadows of these stones to tell the time and study astronomy. Many of these stones weigh up to 50,000 kilograms – almost seven times the weight of an African elephant!

FACT FILE

UNITED KINGDOM OF GREAT BRITAIN AND NORTHERN IRELAND

Capital: London

Population: 66,836,327

Language: English

Currency: British pound

Area: 244,820 square kilometres

Major Industries: machine tools, electric power equipment, railroad equipment, shipbuilding, aircraft, motor vehicles, electronics, metals, chemicals, coal, petro-leum, paper products, food processing, textiles, clothing, consumer goods

BRITISH ISLES

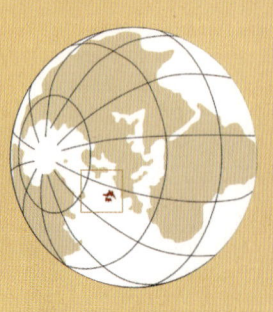

The United Kingdom and the Republic of Ireland together make up the British Isles. England, Scotland, Wales and Northern Ireland form the United Kingdom. England is the biggest and most densely populated region in the British Isles. London, its cosmopolitan capital, has over 7 million people. A mild, wet climate makes most of the British Isles fertile; about three-quarters of the land is used for farming. Grain, fruit and vegetables are grown here. Cattle are reared for meat and dairy products. Cheddar cheese is named after the Cheddar village in Somerset, where it was traditionally made. In the 1800s, some of the world's earliest factories for textiles, steel and shipbuilding were set up in Britian. Now industries like electronics, chemicals, tourism and banking are important.

North Sea

Oil rig

Moray Firth

Fishing industry

Aberdeen

Oil

Scottish man

Arctic terns

ST ANDREWS BAY

Newcastle upon Tyne

Juniper wood

PEN

Dennis the Menace

Dundee

Edinburgh

GRAMPIAN MTS

Whiskey cask

Sheep

Long-horned highland cattle

Edinburgh Castle

Tweed

Cattle

SOUTHERN UPLAND

SCOTLAND

Glasgow Cathedral

Glasgow

Oil

Scots pine trees

SHETLAND ISLANDS

Puffin

Lerwick

Fish

ORKNEY ISLANDS

Fish

Skibo Castle

White-water rafting

Red deer

Skiing

NORTH WEST HIGHLANDS

MT BEN NEVIS 1,343 m

Mull

Lewis

Skye

North Uist

South Uist

Inner Hebrides

Islay

Arran

Northern Cha

NORTHERN IRELAND

Sheep

Londonderry

ATLANTIC OCEAN

Northern

Fishing trawler

Oil rig

N

STRAIT OF DOVER

English Channel

CHANNEL ISLANDS

Celtic Sea

Irish Sea

CARDIGAN BAY

Bristol Channel

Isles of Scilly

Fish

Fishing trawler

UNITED KINGDOM

ENGLAND

WALES

IRELAND

CUMBRIAN MTS

CAMBRIAN MTS

Belfast
Dublin
Waterford
Limerick
Cork

Middlesbrough
York
Leeds
Sheffield
Blackpool
Preston
Manchester
Liverpool
Nottingham
Birmingham
Stratford-upon-Avon
Oxford
Bristol
Cardiff
Swansea
Cheddar
Exeter
Plymouth
Southampton
Portsmouth
Bournemouth
Brighton
Dover
Southend-On-Sea
London
Cambridge
Ipswich
Norwich
Kingston-Upon-Hull

Isle of Man
Douglas
Isle of Anglesey

300 Kilometres
250
200
150
100
50
0

150 Miles
120
90
60
30
0

FESTIVALS AND FAIRS

Trooping the Colour is the celebration of the British monarch's birthday. This parade is held every year in June in London. The current Queen was born in April in London, but the celebration has always been held in June for all kings and queens for over a hundred years.

The Republic of Ireland occupies the greater part of the island of Ireland. The Atlantic coastline, the mountains and rich farmlands inspired various names for the country – such as the 'Emerald Isle' and the poetic 'Erin'.

FACT FILE

ENGLAND
Capital: London
Population: 49,138,831
Language: English
Currency: British pound
Highest Mountain: Scafell Pike (978 metres)
Major Industries: Banking and finance, steel, tourism, food processing, textiles, car making

WALES
Capital: Cardiff
Population: 2,903,085
Language: English
Currency: British pound
Area: 20,758 square kilometres
Highest Mountain: Snowdon (1,085 metres)
Major Industries: Iron and steel, fishing, mining, tourism

SCOTLAND
Capital: Edinburgh
Population: 5,062,011
Language: English
Currency: British pound
Area: 78,789 square kilometres
Highest Mountain: Ben Nevis (1,343 metres)

Major Industries: Oil drilling, natural gas, whiskey processing, fishing, tourism, car making

NORTHERN IRELAND
Capital: Belfast
Population: 1,685,267
Language: English
Currency: British pound
Area: 14,160 square kilometres
Highest Peak: Slieve Donard (852 metres) in the Mourne Mountains
Major Industries: Textiles, tourism, shipbuilding, fishing

REPUBLIC OF IRELAND
Capital: Dublin
Population: 3,883,159
Languages: Gaelic and English
Currency: Euro (previously - Irish pound)
Area: 70,280 square kilometres
Highest Peak: Carrantoohill (1,041 metres) in the Macgillycuddy's Reeks
Major Industries: Software, food processing, beer processing, fishing, textiles, tourism

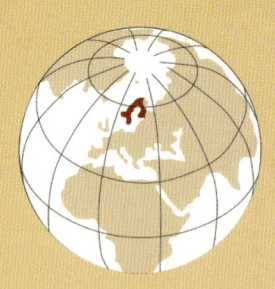

SCANDINAVIA

Sweden, Norway, Denmark, Finland and the island of Iceland are often together known as Scandinavia. Finland is rich in forests and lakes, Sweden and Norway are mountainous for the most part and Denmark is largely flat, with rolling plains. Iceland, the second largest island in Europe, has huge glaciers as well as active volcanoes. It has more hot springs than any other place in the world. It is known as the Land of Ice and Fire. Northern Scandinavia lies in the Arctic Circle. In midsummer it has light for 24 hours of the day and is known as the Land of the Midnight Sun. For centuries, skiing was the main way to travel through the snowbound region. The oldest pair of wooden skis in the world has been found in Scandinavia. Skiing remains a favourite winter sport. The world's longest cross-country ski race takes place in Finland every year.

FESTIVALS AND FAIRS

The Norway Constitution Day is celebrated on the 17th of May every year. It is a day of flags, parades, speeches and bands playing the national anthem. Everywhere the people wear their embroidered national costume called 'bunad'.

Beluga whales

Puffin

Godafoss waterfall

Geyser

ICELAND

Narwhals

Vatnajokull glacier

Reykjavik

Fish

| 0 | 100 | 200 | 300 | 400 | 500 Kilometres |
| 0 | 50 | 100 | 150 | 200 | 250 | 300 Miles |

FLORA AND FAUNA

In Finland, the lily-of-the-valley is the national flower. This bell-shaped, fragrant wild flower is used as a decoration on festive occasions. It is also used to make perfumes and medicines.

Reindeer live in Norway and Sweden. These animals, with big antlers, are found in herds of hundreds. The Samis, who are the native of northern Scandinavia, rear the reindeer for meat, milk and hides. The traditional Sami house is a tent made of reindeer skin.

ATLANTIC OCEAN

Walrus

Alesund

Mt GALDHOPIC
2,469 m

Christmas trees

Bergen

Odda

Fishing industry

Parliament building

Stavanger

Arendal

Birch trees

Kristiansand

Viking ship

Oil rig

Skagerrak

Kattegat

North Sea

Alborg

Pigs

Jazz trumpet

DENMARK

Esbjerg

Oil rig

Dairy

Odense

Danish pastry

Windsurfing

GERMANY

Lolland

MAN-MADE LANDMARK

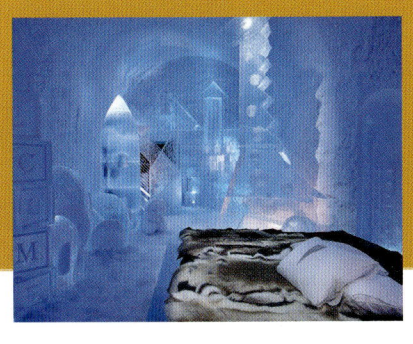

The Ice Hotel in Lapland, in northern Scandinavia, is made of snow and ice. Even the beds are made of ice! This unique place is decorated with ice sculptures. There is an ice church too. The Ice Hotel melts down into a river every summer and is rebuilt in winter.

FACT FILE

REPUBLIC OF FINLAND

Capital: Helsinki
Population: 5,521,606
Languages: Finnish and Swedish
Currency: Euro (previously – Markka)
Area: 337,030 square kilometres
Major Industries: Metal products, pulp and paper, copper, electronics, textiles, chemicals

KINGDOM OF SWEDEN

Capital: Stockholm
Population: 10,278,887
Language: Swedish
Currency: Swedish Krona
Area: 449,964 square kilometres
Major Industries: Automobiles, iron and steel, precision equipment, processed foods

KINGDOM OF NORWAY

Capital: Oslo
Population: 5,347,896
Language: Norwegian
Currency: Norwegian Krone
Area: 324,220 square kilometres
Major industries: Fishing, paper production, shipbuilding, timber, metals, chemicals, petroleum and natural gas

KINGDOM OF DENMARK

Capital: Copenhagen
Population: 5,814,422
Language: Danish
Currency: Danish Krone
Area: 43,094 square kilometres

Major industries: Shipbuilding, fishing, textiles, food processing, furniture, construction, chemical products

REPUBLIC OF ICELAND

Capital: Reykjavik
Population: 360,563
Language: Icelandic
Currency: Icelandic Króna
Area: 103,000 square kilometres
Major industries: Fish processing, geothermal power, tourism

Map labels

North Cape
Hammerfest
Barents Sea
VESTERÅLEN
LOPPHAVET
Alta
Vadsø
LOFOTEN ISLANDS
Tromsø
Sami tribe
Reindeer
Norwegian Sea
Puffin
Fish
Dog-sledding
Narvik
Fox
LAPPLAND
Gold
RUSSIAN FEDERATION
Sheep
Timber
Copper
Birch tree
KJØLEN MTS
Brown bear
Elk
Steel industry
Diamonds
Namsos
Haparanda
Skiing
Sami tribe
Copper
Santa Claus
Iron ore
Paper industry
Yachting
Oulu
Pine trees
Trondheim
Cycling
Umeå
Lead
FINLAND
NORWAY
SWEDEN
Kokkola
Brown bear
Musk ox
Ice hockey
Vaasa
Kayaking
Red deer
Hedgehog
Gold
Dairy
Seals
Apples
Timber
PÄIJÄNNE
Trout
Vigeland Park
Swedish meatballs
Tampere
Mikkeli
SAIMAA
Oslo
Falun
Fishing boats
Nokia industry
Paper industry
Potatoes
Turku
Helsinki
Karlstad
Car industry
ÅLAND ISLANDS
Hanko
Senate Square
GULF OF FINLAND
Örebro
Stockholm
Fish
LAKE VÄNERN
Wheat
Volvo car
Aircraft industry
GULF OF BOTHNIA
ESTONIA
Göteborg
Boras
Fishing trawler
Slite
Gotland
Textile industry
Borgholm
Lighthouse
Öland
Sugar beet
Pigs
Baltic Sea
Halmstad
Helsingborg
Malmö
LATVIA
LITHUANIA
BELARUS

FRANCE, GERMANY, AUSTRIA & SWITZERLAND

This part of the world has a rich heritage of history, tradition and culture. It has produced great painters, musicians, writers and thinkers. Each of the regions has very distinct customs and cuisine. France and Germany have many big industries. Switzerland and Austria are small countries situated on the Alps. A part of this range runs through eastern France and southern Germany. All these countries have thick timber-growing forests. The mountains have lush cattle pastures. The French make over 400 kinds of cheese; they are also known for their perfumes. Swiss chocolates are famous all over the world, while Austria is known for its creamy cakes. Excellent wines come from French and German vineyards. Paris, the French capital, leads the world in fashion and art. Vienna is well known for its opera houses and coffee.

FLORA AND FAUNA

Vast expanses of land in France are covered with vineyards. Grapes grown here are used to make the famous French wines. Roses are also planted in vineyards. The health of the flowers tells the farmer if the grapes are growing well!

The ibex is a mountain goat that lives in the Swiss Alps. It has long, curved horns. The ibex is an excellent mountain climber.

FESTIVALS AND FAIRS

Zibele-Märit, or Onion Market, dates back to the 1500s. It is a day-long festival held in Bern, Switzerland, in November. Stalls sell plaited strings of onions and onion sculptures and people roam the streets wearing onion costumes.

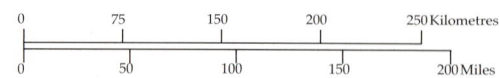

UNITED

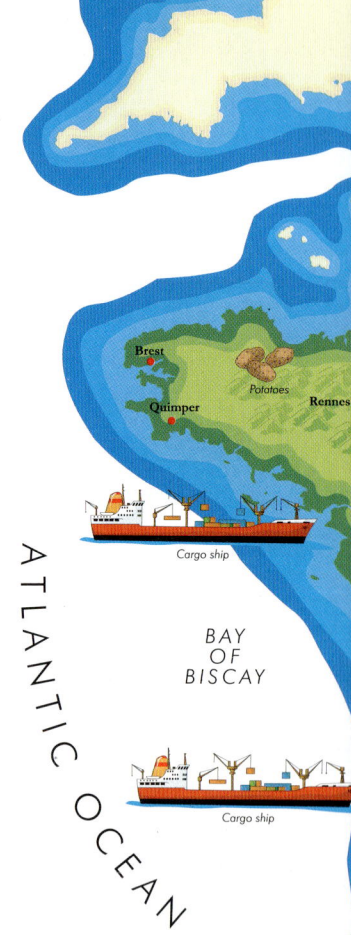

Brest

Quimper

Potatoes

Rennes

Cargo ship

ATLANTIC OCEAN

BAY OF BISCAY

Cargo ship

FACT FILE

FRANCE

Capital: Paris
Population: 67,248,926
Language: French
Currency: Euro (previously – French franc)
Area: 545,630 square kilometres

FEDERAL REPUBLIC OF GERMANY

Capital: Berlin
Population: 83,092,962
Language: German
Currency: Euro (previously – Deutschemark)
Area: 357,000 square kilometres

FEDERAL REPUBLIC OF AUSTRIA

Capital: Vienna
Population: 8,879,920
Language: German
Currency: Euro (previously – Austrian Schilling)
Area: 83,858 square kilometres

SWISS CONFEDERATION (SWITZERLAND)

Capital: Bern
Population: 8,575,280
Languages: German, French and Italian
Currency: Swiss Franc
Area: 41,290 square kilometres

MAN-MADE LANDMARK

The Eiffel Tower was built by Gustave Eiffel in 1889, for the Paris World's Fair. Popularly called the 'Iron Lady', the 324-metre tall tower has more than 1,600 steps to take visitors to the top. Over 200 million people so far have visited the Eiffel Tower.

FESTIVALS AND FAIRS

The Schueberfouer Fair is held every August in Luxembourg. The fair begins with the Hämmelsmarsch, a march of sheep decorated with colourful ribbons. A shepherd and his flock of sheep is followed by a music band along the streets. There are stalls selling food, pottery and cattle at the fair.

THE NETHERLANDS

WEST FRISIAN ISLANDS

WADDENZEE

North Sea

IJSSELMEER

Tobacco industry
Printing industry
Natural gas
Groningen
Enschede
Paper industry
Soccer
Wadlopen
Leeuwarden
Cheese
Zwolle
IJSSEL
Cycling
Wild boar
Friesian cow
Fishing industry
Eel
Windsurfing
Arnhem
Textile industry
Red deer
RHINE
Cheese
Diamonds
Television broadcast
Haarlem-Amsterdamse
Poort
Haarlem
Amsterdam
Utrecht
Ice hockey
Tulips
The Hague
Blue pottery
Rotterdam
Catamaran race
Cargo ship

FLORA AND FAUNA

The Netherlands is the largest exporter of flowers and flower bulbs in the world. Daffodils, hyacinths, and tulips grow very well in the cool Dutch climate.

The Dutch rear herds of black-and-white Friesian cows. Their milk is used to make a variety of cheeses, the most famous of which is the wax-covered Edam with its distinct red colour.

LOW COUNTRIES

The Netherlands (or Holland), Belgium, and Luxembourg are together called the Low Countries. Much of this region is flat and lies below sea level. Luxembourg and the wooded Ardennes Hills in southern Belgium are the only highlands. Most of the land in The Netherlands was once covered with water.

The water was pumped out and is now kept at bay by sand dunes and dikes. Some cities, like Amsterdam, have waterways that freeze during winter, creating a vast ice floor for skating. Cycling is the most popular sport as well as a means of travel in the region. Belgium has one of the world's densest railway networks. A heavily industrialised country, Belgium also makes some of the best chocolates anywhere! Luxembourg, a country of rolling farmlands and woods, is also very wealthy.

FACT FILE

KINGDOM OF THE NETHERLANDS
Capital: Amsterdam
Population: 17,344,874
Language: Dutch
Currency: Euro (previously - Guilder)
Area: 41,526 square kilometres
Major Industries: Agriculture, horticulture, shipping, electronics, banking

KINGDOM OF BELGIUM
Capital: Brussels
Population: 11,488,980
Languages: French, German and Dutch
Currency: Euro (previously - Franc)
Area: 30,528 square kilometres
Major Industries: Agriculture, car making, textiles, food, iron and steel, diamond cutting

GRAND DUCHY OF LUXEMBOURG
Capital: Luxembourg
Population: 620,001
Language: Luxembourgish
Currency: Euro (previously - Luxembourg Franc)
Area: 2,586 square kilometres
Major Industries: Iron and steel, electrical equipment, rubber, banking

MAN-MADE LANDMARK

The Peace Palace in The Hague is the seat of the International Court of Justice. The 20th-century building was built with money donated by Andrew Carnegie, the American philanthrophist. Decorated with gifts from all over the world, the building also houses a splendid library.

FLORA AND FAUNA

The warm and dry climate of southern Italy is perfect for growing olives. Olives are green but take on a violet-black shade as they ripen. Olives are an important part of Italian food. Olive oil is used for cooking, treating sunburn, and making certain cosmetics.

The wolf, or the il lupu, is found in the Alps and the Apennines. This hunter buries pieces of meat under the ground, only to eat them weeks later. Legend has it that Romulus and Remus, the founders of Rome, were brought up by a she-wolf, who had saved them from drowning.

ITALY & MALTA

Italy is shaped like a boot that juts out into the Mediterranean Sea. Sicily, Sardinia, and a number of other smaller islands are a part of Italy. The Alps run along northern Italy, which experiences colder winters than the rest of the country. Southern Italy has a sunny and warm Mediterranean climate. The Vatican City State, the smallest country in the world, and San Marino are two independent countries that lie within Italy. The Vatican City is situated within the city of Rome. Venice, the city of canals and gondolas, is in the north. Apples, pears, and tomatoes are grown in the Po Valley. While the pizza originated in Italy, the idea of making pasta came from noodles brought from China. Another famous product is Chianti, a wine made in the hilly vineyards of central Italy.

FESTIVALS AND FAIRS

The Race of the Candles, held in Gubbio in the month of May, has three teams of men running through the narrow streets of the town, up to Mt Ingino. Each team carries a giant wooden candle with a small statue of the town's patron saint. The team that finishes with the statue standing upright is the winner.

MAN-MADE LANDMARK

The Colosseum, built over 1900 years ago in Rome, is one of the seven wonders of the ancient world. This large amphitheatre could seat over 50,000 people. The ancient Romans came to the Colosseum to watch specially-trained men, called gladiators, fight fierce animals such as lions.

Situated between Europe and Africa, the Mediterranean island of Malta is a hilly country, home to a diverse group of Arabs, Normans, Sicilians and English.

SICILY
Mt ETNA 3,340 m
Catania
Syracuse
Cotton
Ragusa
Agrigento
Maize
Wine
Citrus fruits
Fishing trawler
STRAIT OF SICILY
Pantelleria
Gozo
Valletta
MALTA
Cargo ship

Mediterranean Sea

400 Kilometres
200 Miles
0 50 100 150 200 300
0 100 200 300 400

FACT FILE

ITALY

Capital: Rome
Population: 59,729,081
Language: Italian
Currency: Euro (earlier – Lira)
Area: 301,250 square kilometres
Major Industries: Car making, textiles, footwear, electronics, food processing, tourism

REPUBLIC OF MALTA

Capital: Valletta
Population: 504,062
Language: Maltese
Currency: Maltese Lira
Area: 316 square kilometres
Major Industries: Tourism, ship building, electronics

THE REPUBLIC OF SAN MARINO
Capital: San Marino
Population: 33,864
Language: Italian
Currency: Euro (earlier – Lira)
Area: 61 square kilometres
Major Industries: Tourism, clothing, banking

STATE OF THE VATICAN CITY

Capital: Vatican City
Population: 800
Language: Italian
Currency: Euro, Vatican Lira
Area: 0.44 square kilometres
Major Industries: Tourism, textiles, printing

1
2
3
4
5
6
7
8
9
10
11
12
13
14
15

FESTIVALS AND FAIRS

In Greece, every February and March, three weeks before Lent, the Greek Carnival is celebrated. Each city celebrates the carnival with parades, traditional dancing, feasting and colourful costumes.

N

CENTRAL EASTERN EUROPE

Eastern Europe covers more than 13 countries. The region is mostly mountainous, except in Poland, Hungary and parts of the Czech Republic. Poland has vast plains, lakes and marshes, and much of the Czech Republic has flat farmland. The beautiful, old capital city of Prague is often called Zlata Praha, or the Golden Prague, because of its churches with gilded roofs. Maize, wheat, potatoes and sugar beet grow in Hungary's rich, black soil. Eastern Europe has large reserves of coal and oil. Romania produces the largest amount of crude oil. Its forests are a rich source of timber. Greece, in the south of the Balkan Peninsula, has over 1,400 islands. Greece is also the seat of the first great European civilization and is well known for its ancient monuments.

Baltic Sea

LITHUANIA

BELORUSSIA

UKRAINE

MOLDOVA

Black Sea

Sea of

GERMANY

POLAND

Szczecin
Gdansk
Bydgoszcz
Poznan
Warsaw
Lublin
Krakow

Cargo ship
Kayaking
Tourism
Dairy
Potatoes
Oak tree
Polish folk doll
Steel industry
Wroclaw
Electronics
MASURIAN LAKES
Deer
Wolf
Apples
Timber
Textile industry
Iron ore
Coal
Sugar beet
Barley
Natural gas

CZECHIA

Prague
Brno
Astronomical clock
Beer
Uranium
Coal

AUSTRIA

SLOVAKIA

Bratislava
Hydro-electric dam
Chess
Timber
Tobacco
Wheat
Tourism
Dairy

HUNGARY

Budapest
Szeged
LAKE BALATON
Hungarian folk dance
Sugar beet
Deer
Wheat
Paper industry
Sunflowers
TISZA

SLOVENIA

Ljubljana
Uranium
Chemical industry

CROATIA

Zagreb
Electronics
Iron ore
Petroleum industry
SAVA
Vineyards
DRAVA

BOSNIA & HERZEGOVINA

Sarajevo
Iron ore
Timber
Dairy
Grapes
LAKE SKADAR

MONTENEGRO

Adriatic Sea

SERBIA

Belgrade
Novi Sad
Nis
Pepper
Cabbage
Textile industry
DANUBE

KOSOVO

Lead
Wine
Tobacco
LAKE PRESPA

MACEDONIA (F.Y.R.O.M.)

Skopje
Wheat
Tirane

ALBANIA

ROMANIA

Bucharest
Brasov
Sibiu
Constanta
Chemical industry
Oil
Coal
Car industry
Wild boar
Natural gas
Timber
Pine trees
Golf
Wine
CARPATHIAN MTS
Wheat
Tourism
DANUBE
PRUT

BULGARIA

Sofia
Plovdiv
Burgas
Vineyards
Sheep
Wine
Tobacco
BALKAN MTS
Roses
White stork
Textile industry

Thessaloniki

ITALY

Fish

52

MAN-MADE LANDMARK

The Parthenon is a temple that was built over 2,400 years ago, atop a hill overlooking the city of Athens. The ancient Greeks had made this temple to house a gold-and-ivory statue of Athena, the goddess of wisdom and warfare. Today, the magnificent marble building is in ruins.

FLORA AND FAUNA

Damask roses grow in the Valley of Roses in Bulgaria. Attar, or rose oil, extracted from these roses, is used in perfumes and cosmetics. One drop of attar is made from about 30 roses!

The Bialowieza National Park in Poland is home to the European bison, the largest mammal in Europe. The bison can be over 2 metres tall – taller than an average-sized human.

Map labels

TURKEY

GREECE

Aegean Sea
Ionian Sea
Mediterranean Sea

CYCLADES ISLANDS
DODECANESE ISLANDS
Rhodes
Figs
Fish
Windsurfing
Fishing trawler
Dolphins
Herbs
Olives
Wine
Olives
Tourism
Vineyards
Oranges
Athens
Petroleum industry
Cargo ship
Dolphins
Porpoise
Squid

CRETE
Iraklion
Octopus
Octopus
Tourism

500 Kilometres
300 Miles
0 100 200 300 400 500
0 50 100 150 200 250 300

FACT FILE

REPUBLIC OF POLAND
Capital: Warsaw
Population: 37,965,475
Language: Polish

ROMANIA
Capital: Bucharest
Population: 19,371,648
Language: Romanian

CZECHIA
Capital: Prague
Population: 10,698,896
Language: Czech

MONTENEGRO
Capital: Podgorica
Population: 621,718
Language: Montenegrin

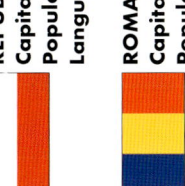
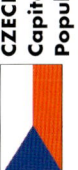

SERBIA
Capital: Belgrade
Population: 6,908,224
Language: Serbian

REPUBLIC OF HUNGARY
Capital: Budapest
Population: 9,749,763
Language: Hungarian

HELLENIC REPUBLIC (GREECE)
Capital: Athens
Population: 10,715,549
Language: Greek

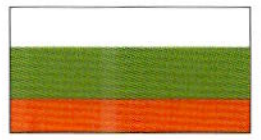

REPUBLIC OF BULGARIA
Capital: Sofia
Population: 6,927,288
Language: Bulgarian

KOSOVO
Capital: Pristina
Population: 1,775,378
Language: Albanian, Serbian

SLOVAK REPUBLIC
Capital: Bratislava
Population: 5,458,827
Language: Slovak

REPUBLIC OF CROATIA
Capital: Zagreb
Population: 4,047,200
Language: Croatian

FEDERATION OF BOSNIA & HERZEGOVINA
Capital: Sarajevo
Population: 3,280,815
Language: Serbo-Croatian

REPUBLIC OF ALBANIA
Capital: Tirana
Population: 2,837,743
Language: Albanian

NORTH MACEDONIA
(Former Yugoslav Republic)
Capital: Skopje
Population: 2,083,380
Languages: Macedonian, Albanian, Turkish, Bosnian

REPUBLIC OF SLOVENIA
Capital: Ljubljana
Population: 2,100,126
Language: Slovene

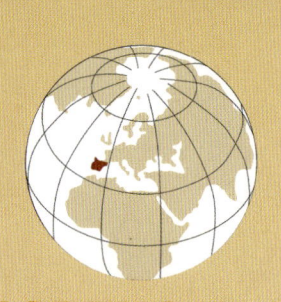

PORTUGAL & SPAIN

Spain and Portugal lie in the southwest of Europe. The Pyrenees, a massive mountain range, separates the two countries from the rest of the continent. The small country of Andorra lies in the Pyrenees valleys. It has lofty mountains, high tablelands, or mesetas, and fertile plains. In the south, there are sunny beaches, vineyards, and olive and orange orchards. Barcelona is the main port. Portugal lies to the west of Spain. The northern region is rocky while the south is flat. Spain and Portugal have a long seafaring history. In about the early 16th century, Portuguese sailor Domingo Fernandez Pereira was believed to have been the first European to land on the island of Mauritius. In the 15th century, another Portuguese, Vasco da Gama, discovered the sea route from Europe to India. A Spanish sailor, Christopher Columbus, reached America in 1492.

ATLANTIC OCEAN

N

Fish

La Coruña
Petroleum industry
Apples
Gijon
Steel industry
Fishing trawler
Santander
Santiago
Copper
Coal
Leon
Corn
Chemical industry
Vine
Burgos
Vigo
Vineyards
Sheep
Wheat
Olives
Cattle
Braga
Gold
Valladolid
Porto
Port wine
DOURO
Cattle
SPAIN
Rye
Cork
Salamanca
Spanish omelette
Avila
Soccer
Olives
Potatoes
Footwear
Uranium
Madrid
Coimbra
Cork
Apparel industry
Toledo
TAGUS (TEJO)
PORTUGAL
Rice
Corn
Vineyards
Olives
Pigs
Steel industry
Oil
Cork
Mérida
Flamenco dance
Lisbon
GUADIANA
Badajoz
Setúbal
Sheep
Azulejos painted tiles
Gold
Tomatoes
Fish
Portuguese folk dancers
Oranges
Cordoba
GUADALQUIVIR
Golf
Plaza de España
Lead
Sherry wine
Cargo ship
Pigs
Seville
Felipe V Gate
Grana
Tourism
Faro
Bullfighting
Málaga
Cargo ship
Cádiz
Onions
Gibraltar (UK)
Barbary Macaque
STRAIT OF GIBRALTAR

FLORA AND FAUNA

The cork oak tree grows in plenty in the sunny, southern parts of Portugal. The tree has a thick bark, which is used to make cork. Cork is mainly used to make bottle stoppers. Portugal produces more cork than any other country.

The only wild monkeys in Europe, the Barbary macaques, are found in the British colony of the Rock of Gibraltar. These monkeys have almost no tail. They have cheek pouches that store food.

FESTIVALS AND FAIRS

La Tomatina, the popular tomato throwing festival, is celebrated in August, in the Spanish town of Bunol. Thousands of people gather in the town's main square to hurl gooey, squishy tomatoes at each other, all in good fun.

BAY OF BISCAY

FRANCE

ANDORRA
Andorra La Vella

PYRENEES

San Sebastián
Bilbao
Paper industry
Vitoria
Pamplona
Bullfighting
Iron ore
EBRO
Chemical industry
Zaragoza
Sugar beet
DUERO (DOURO)
Spanish guitar
Timber
Oranges
White wine
EBRO
Rice
Pears
Apples
Car industry
Barcelona
Textile industry
Tarragona
Oil rig

Costa Brava
Costa Dorada

GULF OF VALENCIA

Car industry
Bullfighting
Cotton
Wheat
Footwear
Valencia
Textile industry
Sunflowers
Wine
Alicante
Tourism
Olives
Citrus fruits
Murcia
Lorca
Cartagena
The Alhambra Palace
Almería
Fish

Cruise liner

Costa Blanca

Mediterranean Sea

BALEARIC ISLANDS
Menorca
Mahón
Palma
Figs
Mallorca
Ibiza
Ibiza

MAN-MADE LANDMARK

Alhambra Castle

The Alhambra ('Red Castle') has stood at the southern city of Granada for more than 700 years. It was built by the Muslim rulers of Spain. The large complex was divided into an alcazaba (fortress), an alcázar (palace) and a medina (city). In olden times, rulers, courtiers and soldiers of high rank lived in the Alhambra.

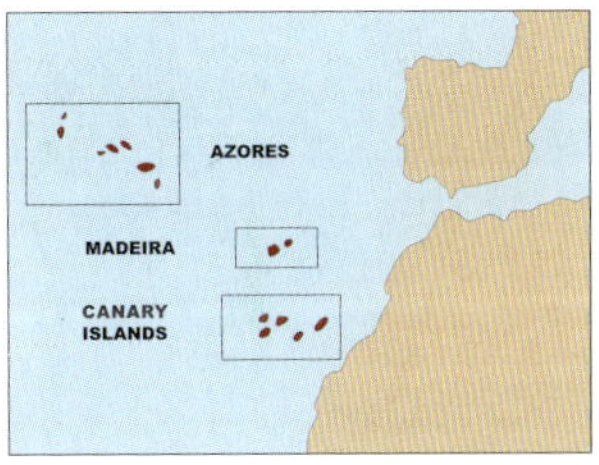

AZORES (PORTUGAL)
Corvo
Flores
Graciosa
Terceira
Faial
Pico
Vineyards
Sao Miguel
Ponta Delgada
Santa Maria

AZORES
MADEIRA
CANARY ISLANDS

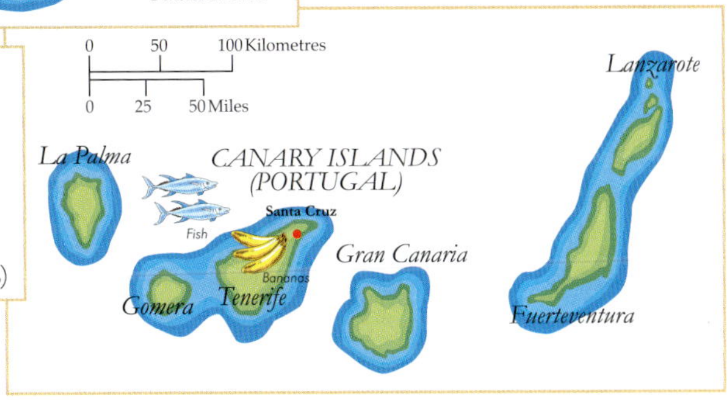

MADEIRA (PORTUGAL)
Madeira wine
Funchal

0   50   100 Kilometres
0   25   50 Miles

Lanzarote
La Palma
CANARY ISLANDS (PORTUGAL)
Santa Cruz
Fish
Bananas
Gran Canaria
Gomera
Tenerife
Fuerteventura

0   50   150   200   250   300 Kilometres
0   30   60   90   120   150 Miles

FACT FILE

KINGDOM OF SPAIN

Capital: Madrid
Population: 47,351,567
Language: Castilian Spanish
Currency: Euro (previously – Spanish peseta)
Area: 504,782 square kilometres
Major Industries: Shipbuilding, textiles, beverages, steel, chemicals, tourism

REPUBLIC OF PORTUGAL

Capital: Lisbon
Population: 10,305,564
Language: Portuguese
Currency: Euro (previously – Portuguese escudo)
Area: 92,391 square kilometres
Major Industries: Agriculture, wood products, textiles, footwear, wine making, food processing, chemicals, oil refining, tourism

PRINCIPALITY OF ANDORRA

Capital: Andorra la Vella
Population: 77,265
Language: Catalan
Currency: Euro (previously – French franc, Spanish peseta)
Area: 468 square kilometres
Major Industries: Tourism, timber products, tobacco, banking

AFRICA

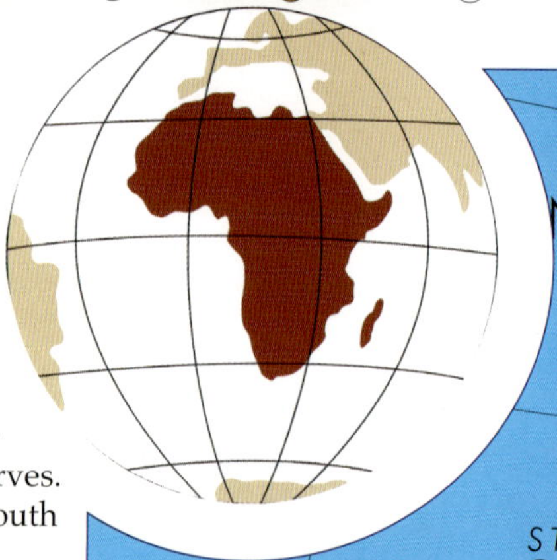

Africa is the second largest continent, with more than fifty countries. The Equator runs through its middle, which is why most of the continent is very hot. The Sahara, the largest desert on earth, covers one-third of the continent. East Africa is made up of plateaus. Mt Kenya and Mt Kilimanjaro lie along the Great Rift Valley, which runs from the Red Sea to Mozambique. The world's longest river, the Nile, flows north into the Mediterranean Sea. Huge tropical forests lie in the regions around the Equator, in west and central Africa. Between the rainforests and deserts are the grasslands. The Kalahari and the Namib deserts lie in the south. Africa is home to a wonderful variety of wildlife, including lions, cheetahs and gorillas.

Cocoa, coffee, tea, cotton, cashew nuts and bananas are grown in Africa. Hardwoods like mahogany, from tropical forests, are exported. Countries like Libya and Nigeria have big oil reserves. Diamonds and gold are mined in South Africa, Botswana, Congo and other countries.

Many different tribes live all over Africa. These include the Bushmen and Bedouins of the desert, the Masai in Kenya and Tanzania, and the Zulus in the Natal Province of South Africa. About two-thirds of the world's poorest countries are in Africa. Most Africans live in villages and farms. The Senegal, Volta, Niger and Congo rivers have fertile and densely-populated basins. Big cities have grown along the coastline. Cape Town in South Africa, Lagos on the west coast, Cairo, the capital of Egypt, Nairobi and Casablanca are well-known cities.

Mosque of Abu El Abbas

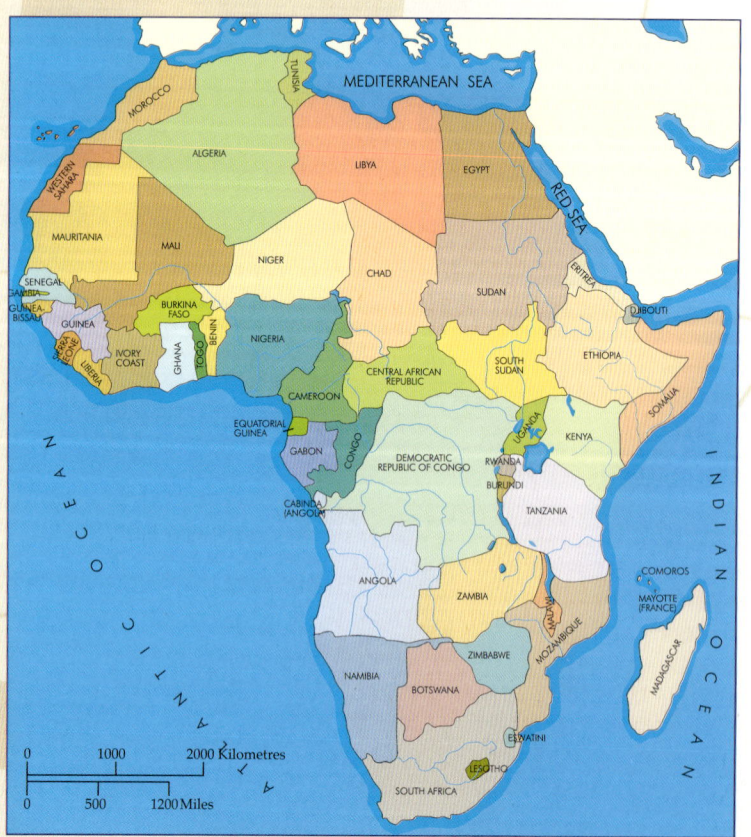

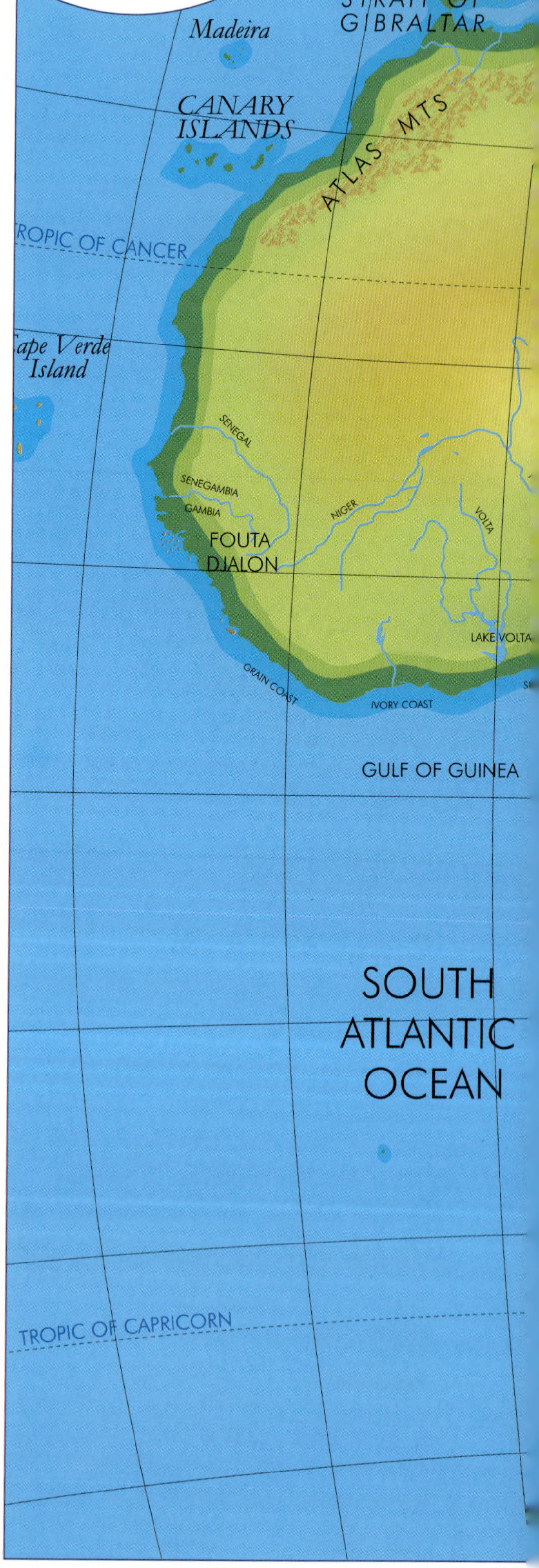

EUROPE

CARPATHIANS

Aral Sea

Black Sea

CAUCASUS

Caspian Sea

DINARIC ALPS

APPENNINES

Adriatic Sea

Corsica

Sardinia

ANATOLIA

ASIA

Mediterranean Sea

Cyprus

SYRIAN DESERT

TIGRIS

EUPHRATES

PERSIAN GULF

LIBYAN DESERT

EGYPT

ARABIAN DESERT

AHAGGAR

NILE

NUBIAN DESERT

Red Sea

ARABIA

SAHARA DESERT

GULF OF ADEN

ATBARA

LAKE CHAD

WADAI

CHARI

BLUE NILE

WHITE NILE

ETHIOPIAN HIGHLANDS

OGADEN DESERT

BENUE

ADAMAWA HIGHLANDS

MASSIF DES MONGOS

BAHR EL FEBEL

GEBEL ON NUBAH

SHABELLE

UELE

RIFT VALLEY

LAKE TURKANA

JUBA

OGOOUE

CONGO (ZAIRE)

CHUTES BOYOMA

CONGO BASIN

KASAI

LUALABA

SANKURU

KASAI

CUANGO

LOMAMI

LAKE VICTORIA

TANA

Mt KILIMANJARO 5,895 m

INDIAN OCEAN

CUANZA

LUNGA

LAKE TANGANYIKA

MWERU

ALDABRA ISLANDS

Zanzibar

Comoros

LUAPULA

LUANGA

BANGWEULU SWAMP

LAKE NYASA

BIE PLATEAU

ZAMBEZI

SHIRE

Mauritius

CUBANGO

CUANDO

ZAMBEZI

Réunion

CUNENE

VICTORIA FALLS

LIMPOPO

MADAGASCAR

NAMIB DESERT

WALVIS BAY

KALAHARI DESERT

VAAL

DRAKENSBERG MTS

Mozambique Channel

ORANGE

Cape of Good Hope

| 0 | 500 | 1000 | 1500 | 2000 | 2500 Kilometres |
| 0 | 300 | 600 | 900 | 1200 | 1500 Miles |

FACT FILE

Largest Desert: Sahara
Longest River: Nile
Highest Peak:
Kilimanjaro (5,895 metres)
Largest Lake: Lake Victoria

Active Volcano: Mount Kartala, Republic of the Comoros
Lowest Point: Lake Assal, Djibouti (156 metres below sea level)
Highest Annual Average Temperature: Dalol, Ethiopia
Lowest Annual Average Temperature: Ifrane, Morocco
Highest Annual Average Rainfall: Debundscha, Cameroon
Lowest Annual Average Rainfall: Wadi Halfa, Sudan
Highest Recorded Temperature:
124.3° F, in El Azizia, Libya
Lowest Recorded Temperature: -11° F, in Ifrane, Morocco
Longest Mountain Range: Atlas Mountains

World Heritage site:
Amphitheatre of El Jem Tunisia

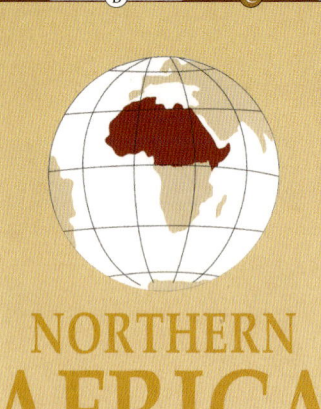

NORTHERN AFRICA

The world's largest desert, the Sahara, stretches across 11 countries in northern Africa. While huge sand dunes and rocky mountains make up most of the desert, there are fertile areas as well. These fertile patches, watered mainly by natural springs, are called oases. Crops such as date palms, wheat, barley, and citrus fruits are grown here. Places that lie close to the Mediterranean Sea are fertile too. The Nile, which is the longest river in the world, flows through Egypt. Most Egyptians live along the river, as the rest of the country is a barren desert. Cotton is grown in plenty around the Nile. Parts of western Africa receive good rainfall, which has helped in the growth of grasslands and lush tropical forests. Rubber, grown in the tropical areas of Nigeria, is a major export.

Map labels

STRAIT OF GIBRALTAR

ATLANTIC OCEAN

Whale shark

N

MOROCCO
Mt TOUBKAL 4,165 m
Tangier
Rabat
Casablanca
Marrakech
Berber tribe
Hand-woven carpet
Olives

Algiers
Sidi-bel-Abbès
Oranges
Olives
Grapes
Barley
TUNISIA
Tuni

ATLAS MTS
Natural gas
Petroleum refinery
Timimoun
ALGERIA

WESTERN SAHARA
Laayoune
Dakhla
African elephant
Lion
Iron ore
Olives
Cattle
Oasis

S A H A R A
AHAGGAR MTS
Ostrich
Scorpion
Livestock
Uranium

MAURITANIA
FISH
Fishing industry
Fishing trawler
Nouakchott
Turtle
Pulses
Maize

MALI
Peanuts
Dates
Timbuktu
Cotton
Rice
Mangoes
Gold
Sugar cane
Mopti Mosque
Baobab trees

NIGER
Niamey
Cowpeas
Cotton
African elephant
Lion
Kano
Bano

SENEGAL
Dakar
GAMBIA
Banjul
GUINEA-BISSAU
Bissau
GUINEA
Conakry
Gemstones

BURKINA FASO
Bamako
Ouagadougou
Fulani tribe
Cocoa beans
Zebu cattle with herdsmen

NIGERIA
Abuja
Marigo
Lagos

SIERRA LEONE
Freetown
Pineapples
Rubber tree

IVORY COAST
Yamoussoukro
Abidjan
Cocoa beans
Timber

LIBERIA
Monrovia
Gold
Diamonds
Dates

GHANA
Accra
Gold
LAKE VOLTA
Yams

TOGO
Lomé
BENIN
Porto Novo
Cocoa beans
Petroleum refinery
Chimpanzee
Port Harcourt
Cotton
Douala
Yao

Fish

GULF OF GUINEA
Turtle

FLORA AND FAUNA

Found in the grassy plains and savannas, the African lion is the most majestic of the entire cat family. Lions live in groups called prides. The lionesses are the hunters while the males are the defenders of the pride and the territory.

Rubber trees grow on the large plantations in Liberia and parts of Nigeria. Farmers cut the bark of the tree to extract a thick liquid called latex, which is used to make rubber.

FACT FILE

 **PEOPLE'S DEMOCRATIC REPUBLIC OF ALGERIA**
Capital: Algiers

 **REPUBLIC OF THE GAMBIA**
Capital: Banjul

 **KINGDOM OF MOROCCO**
Capital: Rabat

 **REPUBLIC OF GUINEA**
Capital: Conakry

 **WESTERN SAHARA**
Capital: El-Aaiún

 **REPUBLIC OF SIERRA LEONE**
Capital: Freetown

 **REPUBLIC OF SENEGAL**
Capital: Dakar

 **TOGOLESE REPUBLIC**
Capital: Lomé

 **REPUBLIC OF CÔTE D'IVOIRE**
Capital: Yamoussoukro

 **REPUBLIC OF LIBERIA**
Capital: Monrovia

MAN-MADE LANDMARK

The Pyramids of Giza were built in northern Egypt over 4,000 years ago. It is believed that the largest of the three pyramids is made of about 2.3 million stone blocks, and took over 20 years to build. It is known as the Great Pyramid. The pyramids were royal tombs wherein the Egyptians buried the preserved bodies of their kings, who were called pharaohs.

FESTIVALS AND FAIRS

The riverside Nigerian town of Argungu holds the annual Argungu Fishing Festival between February and March. Drummers in canoes follow hordes of fishermen, who try to net the largest number of fish. The fishermen make rattling sounds with big gourds filled with seeds, to drive the fish to shallow waters.

Map labels

Mediterranean Sea
Dolphins
Cargo ship
Tripoli
Benghazi
Olives
Dates
Citrus fruits
Petroleum refinery
Alexandria
Port Said
Suez
Cairo
The Sphinx at Giza
Hurghada
Asyut
Cotton
Peanuts
EGYPT
Sebha
Vulture
LIBYA
Oasis
LIBYAN DESERT
Murzuq
Aswan
LAKE NASSER
Scuba-diver with stingray
SAHARA
TIBESTI MASSIF
Red fox
Luxor Temple
Wadi Halfa
Philae Temple
EMI KOUSSI (3,415 m)
Adder
NUBIAN DESERT
Red Sea
Cassava
Dongola
Nile crocodile
Mangoes
Port Sudan
Suakin
Livestock
Caravan
Oil
Atbara
ERITREA
CHAD
El Fasher
SUDAN
Khartoum
Asmera
Rhinoceros
LAKE CHAD
Giraffes
El Obeid
Cotton
White pelican
Mt RAS DASHEN 4,620 m
DJIBOUTI
Djibouti
GULF OF ADEN
Maiduguri
Ndjamena
Cotton
Oryx
BLUE NILE
Coffee beans
Livestock
Berbera
Fishing industry
Cassava
Wau
Peanuts
Hippopotamus
Addis Ababa
Nazret
Gazelle
Sarh
Coffee beans
WHITE NILE
Moundou
Tobacco
African elephant
Juba
ETHIOPIA
Gore
Gold
Gorilla
Butterflies
Bongo
LAKE RUDOLF
Camel
SOMALIA
CENTRAL AFRICAN REPUBLIC
SOUTH SUDAN
Diamonds
Bananas
CAMEROON
Bangui
Mogadishu
Aluminium foil
CONGO
DEMOCRATIC REPUBLIC OF CONGO
UGANDA
KENYA
Ostrich
INDIAN OCEAN
GABON
Kismaayo

Flags legend

REPUBLIC OF GUINEA-BISSAU Capital: Bissau

FEDERAL REPUBLIC OF NIGERIA Capital: Abuja

REPUBLIC OF MALI Capital: Bamako

REPUBLIC OF NIGER Capital: Niamey

ISLAMIC REPUBLIC OF MAURITANIA Capital: Nouakchott

ERITREA Capital: Asmara

REPUBLIC OF CHAD Capital: N'Djamena

SUDAN Capital: Khartoum

REPUBLIC OF TUNISIA Capital: Tunis

SOMALIA Capital: Mogadishu

REPUBLIC OF DJIBOUTI Capital: Djibouti

SOUTH SUDAN Capital: Juba

LIBYA Capital: Tripoli

REPUBLIC OF CAMEROON Capital: Yaoundé

ARAB REPUBLIC OF EGYPT Capital: Cairo

REPUBLIC OF GHANA Capital: Accra

CENTRAL AFRICAN REPUBLIC Capital: Bangui

REPUBLIC OF BENIN Capital: Porto Novo

BURKINA FASO Capital: Ouagadougou

FEDERAL DEMOCRATIC REPUBLIC OF ETHIOPIA Capital: Addis Ababa

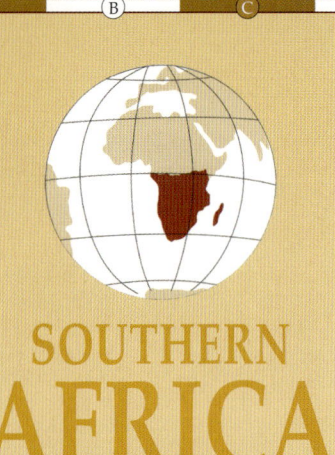

SOUTHERN AFRICA

Southern Africa is a land of hot deserts, dry grasslands, and tropical rainforests. Chimpanzees and leopards are found in the rainforests, while African elephants and giraffes live in the grasslands. The region is rich in metals. The world's deepest gold mine is in South Africa, while Zaire is a leading producer of industrial diamonds. The Great Rift Valley in East Africa is the longest rift in the Earth's crust. Volcanoes and hot springs lie along this crack. The highest African peak, Mt Kilimanjaro in Tanzania, is an extinct volcano. Many African tribes worship this snow-capped mountain. Most tribes are hunter-gatherers, farmers, or cattle herders. The Masai people of East Africa raise cattle for both its milk and blood.

FLORA AND FAUNA

The zebra lives in the African grasslands. This black-and-white-striped animal is called "Quagga" in Afrikaans because of its bray (kwa-ha kwa-ha). No two zebras have the same pattern of stripes.

The baobab tree, found on the dry plains, stores water in its trunk. It is believed that the tree can live to over 1,000 years!

Map

GULF OF GUINEA

Bioko

EQUATORIAL GUINEA · Bata Mbini

SAO TOME AND PRINCIPE

· Libreville

Turtle

Sugar cane

Chimpanzee

GABON

Uranium

Crude oil

Rainforest

Brazzaville · Kinshasa

Cabinda (Angola)

· Matadi

Hydro-electric dam

Cargo ship

Mountain gorilla

Traditional round hut

Coffee

Fish

CONGO

Crocodile

CONGO (ZAIRE)

Mbandaka

Dug-out canoe

African elephant

Kisangani

DEM. REP. OF THE CONGO

CONGO BASIN

Bongo

Nyamuragira volcano

RW

Kigali

Cassava

BU

Gitega

Kananga

Mbuji-Mayi

Blue monkey

Rubber tree

Gold

Diamonds

GREAT RIFT VALLEY

LAKE TANGANYIKA

LAKE MWERU

African elephant

Luanda

Oil

Sunflowers

Malanje

ANGOLA

Diamonds

Copper

Kolwezi

Lubumbashi

LAKE BANGWEULU

Ndola

Benguela

Uranium

Brown hyena

Giraffe

Kabwe

ZAMBIA

Lusaka

Benguela railway

Palm trees

Sá da Bandeira

Iron ore

ZAMBEZI

Victoria Falls

LAKE KARIBA

Mbira

Lion

Copper

Grootfontein

Leopard

ZIMBABWE

Bulawayo

Copper

NAMIBIA

Zebra

Steel industry

LIMPOPO

BOTSWANA

Mahalapye

FISH

Fishing industry

Diamonds

Uranium

Windhoek

Ostrich

Diamonds

Gaborone

KALAHARI DESERT

Car industry

Mbabane

NAMALAND

Gecko

Pretoria

Johannesburg

Natal

NAMIB DESERT

ORANGE

Cotton

Diamonds

Cricket

Gold

Durban

Bloemfontein

Maseru

SOUTH AFRICA

LESOTHO

Umtata

Castle of Good Hope

Grapes

Pineapples

Crabs

Cape Town

Wine

Port Elizabeth

Cape of Good Hope

Whale shark

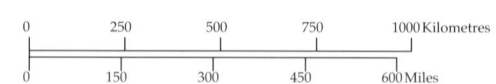

Cargo ship

SOUTH ATLANTIC OCEAN

Fish

N

| 0 | 250 | 500 | 750 | 1000 Kilometres |
| 0 | 150 | 300 | 450 | 600 Miles |

SOMALIA

KENYA

UGANDA
Kampala
Lake Turkana
Cotton
Tea
Cheetah

Masai Mara reserve
Nairobi
Coffee
Masai tribe
Lion
Lake Victoria
Fish

NDA

NDI

Tea
Coffee
Dodoma
Nachingwea
Cocoa beans
Giraffe

Mt Kilimanjaro 5,895 m
Mombasa

Zanzibar
Dar-es-Salaam

TANZANIA
Lake Tanganyika

Mtwara

INDIAN OCEAN

Windsurfing

Cargo ship

Zebra

ALDABRA ISLANDS

MALAWI
Lake Nyasa
Lilongwe
Zomba
Blantyre
Chapel of Nossa Senhora de Baluarte
Lion
Baobab trees
Bananas
African elephant
Coffee
Beira
Sugarcane
Cashew nuts
Maputo
Sugar cane

MOZAMBIQUE

Shrimps
Coral reefs

Humpback whale

Mozambique Channel

ESWATINI

Nacala

Windsurfing

COMOROS
Moroni

Mayotte (Fr)

Flamingos
Cloves
Mangoes
Python
Toamasina

MADAGASCAR

Boabab trees
Iron ore
Antananarivo

Chameleon
Pineapple
Toliara
Gecko

FISH
Fishing industry

MAN-MADE LANDMARK

The 17th-century Castle of Good Hope in Cape Town is the oldest surviving building in South Africa. First built as a clay-and-timber fort by the Dutch, the castle was originally called Fort de Goede Hoop. Later, it was rebuilt as a five-sided stone structure.

FACT FILE

 **REPUBLIC OF EQUATORIAL GUINEA**
Capital: Malabo

REPUBLIC OF MOZAMBIQUE
Capital: Maputo

 **DEMOCRATIC REPUBLIC OF SÃO TOMÉ & PRÍNCIPE**
Capital: São Tomé

REPUBLIC OF ZIMBABWE
Capital: Harare

 GABONESE REPUBLIC
Capital: Libreville

ZAMBIA
Capital: Lusaka

 **REPUBLIC OF CONGO**
Capital: Brazzaville

 **REPUBLIC OF MALAWI**
Capital: Lilongwe

 **DEMOCRATIC REPUBLIC OF THE CONGO**
Capital: Kinshasa

 **BURUNDI**
Capital: Gitega

 **REPUBLIC OF ANGOLA**
Capital: Luanda

 **UNITED REPUBLIC OF TANZANIA**
Capital: Dodoma

 **REPUBLIC OF NAMIBIA**
Capital: Windhoek

 **RWANDA**
Capital: Kigali

 **THE REPUBLIC OF SOUTH AFRICA**
Capital: Pretoria, Cape Town, Bloemfontein

 **REPUBLIC OF KENYA**
Capital: Nairobi

 **KINGDOM OF LESOTHO**
Capital: Maseru

 **REPUBLIC OF UGANDA**
Capital: Kampala

 **KINGDOM OF ESWATINI**
Capital: Mbabane

 **FEDERAL ISLAMIC REPUBLIC OF THE COMOROS**
Capital: Moroni

 **REPUBLIC OF BOTSWANA**
Capital: Gaborone

 **DEMOCRATIC REPUBLIC OF MADAGASCAR**
Capital: Antananarivo

FESTIVALS AND FAIRS

One of the biggest events in Africa is the seasonal migration of a large African antelope called wildebeest. As millions of these animals make their annual journey in April, from the dry grasslands of Tanzania to the greener plains of Kenya, many people gather to see this.

ASIA

Asia is the world's largest continent. It stretches in the north from the Arctic Circle to the Equatorial archipelago, a long chain of more than 13,600 islands. Thirty per cent of the earth's land and sixty percent of its population is in Asia. Found here are dense tropical forests, freezing Arctic regions, deserts and tropical rainforests. The world's highest mountain, Mt Everest at 8,849 m, and the lowest point, the shores of the Dead Sea at 392 m below sea level, are all found in Asia.

The Red Sea and the Suez Canal separate Asia from Africa. It is separated from Europe by the Ural Mountains. The narrow Bering Sea separates Asia from North America. Over 40 independent countries lie in Asia. China and India are the most thickly populated. More than two-thirds of the people in Asia live by farming. Rice is an important crop in most of southern Asia. Tea, coffee, sugar, cotton, tobacco and jute are important crops.

Huge oil reserves are found in south-western Asia - in the desert countries of Saudi Arabia, Kuwait, the United Arab Emirates, Iraq and Iran. Big, crowded cities like Tokyo, Mumbai and Bangkok are some of the largest in the world. Singapore and Hong Kong are important financial centres. Japan manufactures the most cars and televisions in the world, while China has a very rapidly growing economy.

The ancient civilisations of Mesopotamia, China and the Indus Valley, were all born in Asia. Over the centuries, many great empires rose and fell in Asia. From the 1800s, much of the continent was colonised by European countries. Most of these colonised countries have become independent nations. Their economies are becoming stronger. In 1991, the Soviet Union gave up communism and many republics became independent. Asia is a melting pot of cultures with many languages and traditions.

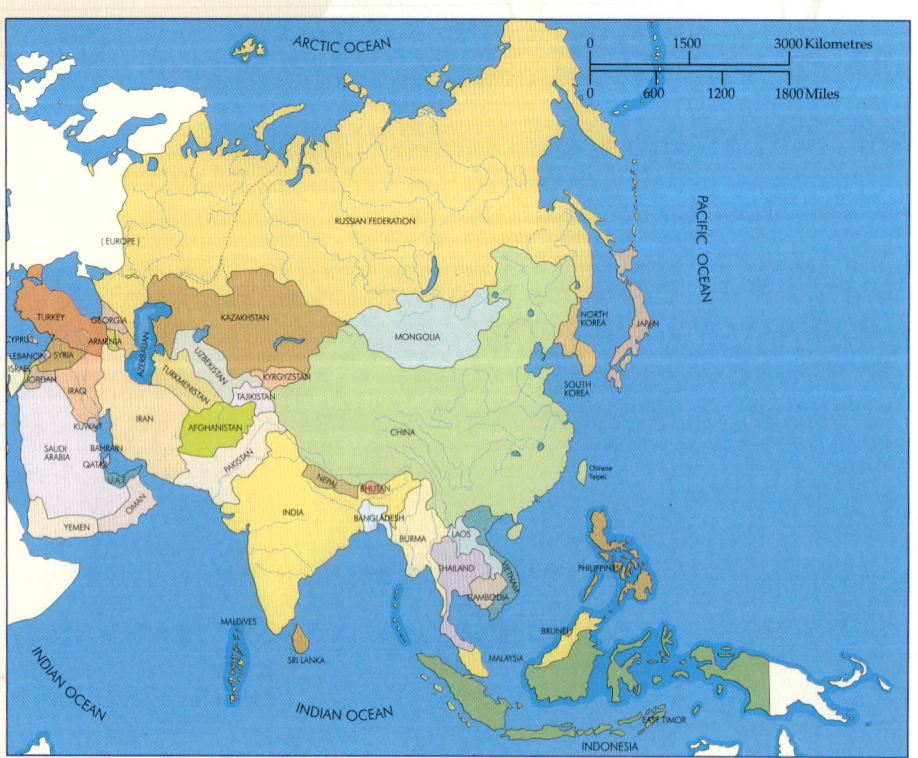

FACT FILE

Longest River: Yangtze
Highest Peak: Mount Everest (8,849 metres)
Largest Desert: Gobi, China
Active Volcano: Mount Krakatau, Indonesia

Kara Sea

Laptev Sea

Bering Sea

NOVAYA ZEMLYA

White Sea

CENTRAL SIBERIAN PLATEAU

EAST SIBERIAN MTS

Sea of Okhotsk

N. DVINA

OB

TUNGUSKA

LENA

KOLYMA

INDIGIRKA

SAKHALIN

U R A L   M T S

WEST SIBERIAN PLAINS

IRTYSH

OB

ALDAN

HOKKAIDO

URAL

TOBOL

AMUR

MANCHURIAN PLAIN

Sea of Japan

HONSHU

KIRGHIZ STEPPE

Aral Sea

SYRDARYA

LAKE BALKHASH

ALTAI MTS

SELENGA

LAKE BAIKAL

ANGARA

G O B I   D E S E R T

Yellow Sea

KYUSHU

CHU

ILI

TIEN SHAN

TARIM BASIN

GREAT PLAINS OF CHINA

East China Sea

TROPIC OF CANCER

AMUDARYA

TAKLA MAKAN

HWANG-HO

HARIRUD

KUNLUN MTS

HINDU KUSH

HELMAND

Chinese Taipei

PACIFIC OCEAN

HIMALAYAS

PLATEAU OF TIBET

▲ MT EVEREST 8,848 m

TSANGPO

YANGZE

MTS

INDUS

THAR DESERT

YAMUNA

BRAHMAPUTRA

GANGES

GULF OF OMAN

NARMADA

HONG

HAINAN

LUZON

Arabian Sea

DECCAN PLATEAU

GODAVARI

SALWEEN

MEKONG

South China Sea

MINDANAO

Philippines Sea

WESTERN GHATS

KRISHNA

EASTERN GHATS

BAY OF BENGAL

IRRAWADDY

LAKSHADWEEP ISLANDS

Celebes Sea

IRIAN JA

MALDIVES

GULF OF THAILAND

MALAY PENINSULA

MOLUCCAS

CELEBES

BORNEO

INDIAN OCEAN

				Kilometres
0	600	1200	1800	2400	
0	300	600	900	1200	1500 Miles

SUMATRA

Java Sea

JAVA

Timor Sea

Largest Lake: Aral Sea
Lowest Point:
Dead Sea shore (-430 metres)
Highest Annual Average Rainfall:
Mawsynram, India
Lowest Annual Average Rainfall:

Aden, Yemen
Highest Recorded Temperature:
129° F, in Tirat Tsvi, Israel
Lowest Recorded Temperature:
-90° F, in Verkhoyansk, Russia

Cityscape of Hong Kong

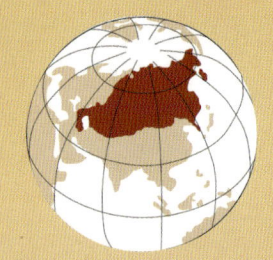

EURASIA

Eurasia stretches from Europe in the west to eastern Asian shores. The northern ice-bound coasts border the Arctic Ocean. Towards the north lies the icy-cold, treeless expanse of the tundra. The world's largest coniferous forest lies below the tundra in the taiga region. The grasslands, or the steppes, are in the southwest. High mountains and deserts lie towards the Chinese border. The Ural Mountains act as a natural divide between east Europe and Russia in the west. Siberia stretches all the way up to the eastern coast. There are over 200 volcanoes. Some of these are active. In 1922, northern Eurasia formed a large communist country called the Soviet Union. Parts of the Soviet Union broke up into several independent countries in 1991. The region has great mineral wealth.

Map labels

POLAND

LITHUANIA
ESTONIA
LATVIA
GULF OF RIGA
Tallinn
Riga
Timber
Amber jewellery
Potatoes
Timber
Dairy
Kaunas
Deer
Vilnius
Poultry
White stock
NEMAN
Potatoes
Glass industry
Chemical industry
Fishing industry
Minsk
BELARUS
Mushroom
Lvov
Sugar beet
Natural gas
Maize
Bison
Pine trees
Elk
Gomel
Pysanka painted eggs
Cossack folk dance
Dairy
Kiev
Barley
ROMANIA
MOLDOVA
Tobacco
Maize
Chisinau
Carved birch box
UKRAINE
Wheat
Oil
Sunflowers
Wheat
Iron ore
Odesa
Coal
Barley
Rye
Kharkiv
Mykolayiv
Sunflowers
Dnepropetrovsk
Steel industry
Oats
Iron ore
Donetsk
Chemical industry
Vineyards
Fishing trawler
Black Sea

0 100 200 300 400 Kilometres
0 75 150 225 300 Miles

Baltic Sea

0 500 1000 1500 2000 Kilometres
0 250 500 750 1000 1250 Miles

POLAND
BELARUS
Alexander
St Basil C
Moscow
UKRAINE
Coal
Iron ore
Black Sea
Rostov-na-Donu
Ballet
Volgograd
Fishing boats
DON
Mt ELBRUS 5,633 m
GEORGIA
Astrakhan
Barley
ARMENIA
Tbilisi
Baku
Yerevan
AZERBAIJAN
Caspian Sea
Oil
Natural
TURKMEN
Ashgabat
Cotton
IRAN
AFGHAN

MAN-MADE LANDMARK

Ivan the Terrible ordered St Basil's Cathedral to be built in the mid-16th century. Situated on the edge of the Red Square in Moscow, this church is topped by onion-shaped domes with colourful, swirling patterns.

FESTIVALS AND FAIRS

In Latvia, St John's Night is celebrated on the longest day of the year in June. Throughout the night, people burn fires, sing, dance, drink beer and eat cheese. Men called Janis wear wreaths made of oak tree leaves on their heads. Couples search for ferns in forests to invoke good luck.

FLORA AND FAUNA

Sugar beet is a white, conical root of a plant. The leafy tops are used as animal feed. Sugar is made from the root. Sugar beet is also eaten as a vegetable.

The endangered Siberian tiger is found in southeastern Siberia, east of the Amur river, and sometimes in Manchuria and Korea. These tigers are paler in colour than most tigers and can blend in with the snowy landscapes.

SWE

LAND

Ostrov Vrangelya

Sea lion

Murmansk

Severnaya Zemlya

Novosibirskiye Ostrova

Novaya Zemlya

Kara Sea

Fishing trawler

Brown bear

Arctic fox

Siberian tiger

Brown bear

Giant otter

rg

Matryoshka dolls

Ballet

Reindeer

Pine tree

Gold

S I B E R I A

Reindeer

Mt KLYUCHEV 4,750 m

Wheat

Textile industry

Gymnastics

Natural gas

Wheat

Timber

Deer

Timber

Magadan

izhiny vgorod

Kirov

Potatoes

Woollen shawl

Carved birch box

Petr Kam

Kazan

Perm

Iron ore

RUSSIAN FEDERATION

Cheetah

Yakutsk

Gold

Sea of Okhotsk

Samara

Yekaterinburg

U R A L MTS

SIBERIAN PLAINS

Diamonds

Elk

Fish

Ufa

Chelyabinsk

Copper

Wild boar

Wheat

Beetroot soup

KU ISL

Caviar

Petropavlovsk

Omsk

Uranium

Timber

Gold

Porcupine

Gold

Pine trees

Coal

Novosibirsk

Krasnoyarsk

Timber

Reindeer

Oil

Khabarovsk

Fishing industry

KAZAKHSTAN

Almola

Astana

Steel industry

Iron ore

Hydroelectric dam

LAKE BAIKAL

ARAL SEA

Chemical industry

Karaganda

Irkutsk

CHINA

Chemical industry

EKISTAN

Sheep

LAKE BALKASH

TIEN SHAN MTS

ALTAI MTS

Vladivostok

Sheep

Wheat

Textile industry

MONGOLIA

Cargo ship

Samarkand

Tashkent

Bishkek

Almaty

Sea of Japan

Dushanbe

KYRGYZSTAN

TAJIKISTAN

PAKISTAN

CHINA

FACT FILE

REPUBLIC OF ARMENIA Capital: Yerevan	**REPUBLIC OF GEORGIA** Capital: Tbilisi	**REPUBLIC OF LITHUANIA** Capital: Vilnius	**TURKMENISTAN** Capital: Ashgabat
REPUBLIC OF AZERBAIJAN Capital: Baku	**REPUBLIC OF KAZAKHSTAN** Capital: Nur-Sultan	**REPUBLIC OF MOLDOVA** Capital: Chisinau	**UKRAINE** Capital: Kiev
REPUBLIC OF BELARUS Capital: Minsk	**KYRGYZ REPUBLIC** Capital: Bishkek	**RUSSIAN FEDERATION** Capital: Moscow	**REPUBLIC OF UZBEKISTAN** Capital: Tashkent
REPUBLIC OF ESTONIA Capital: Tallinn	**REPUBLIC OF LATVIA** Capital: Riga	**REPUBLIC OF TAJIKISTAN** Capital: Dushanbe	

SOUTHWEST ASIA

The Middle East is mostly desert, with high arid mountains to the north. The Mediterranean Sea lies to the west, and towards the south are the Red Sea, Persian Gulf and the Indian Ocean. The fertile land between the Tigris and the Euphrates is the site of the world's oldest civilisation. Christianity, Judaism and Islam arose in the Middle East. The Rub Al Khali ('empty quarter') in Saudia Arabia is the largest sand desert in the world, with dunes as high as 150 metres. This region is scorchingly hot in the summer. The coastal areas are humid and, in the north, the mountains are snow-capped. Oranges, grapefruit, melons, pomegranate and vegetables are grown along the Mediterranean. Date palm trees grow in the oases and places which have some water. The Arab states are wealthy as they produce and export the most oil in the world. Dubai, Bahrain and Muscat are important cities. Ancient cities like Jerusalem and Istanbul attract tourists.

Black Sea

GEORGIA

ARMENIA AZERBAIJAN

Caspian Sea

Textile industry Istanbul
Hagia Sophia
Coal
PONTIC MTS
Bursa
Grapes Ankara
Persian carpets
Izmir
Van cat
TURKEY
Kababs Konya
Cotton TAURUS MTS Citrus fruits
Adana
Eagle
Aleppo
Nicosia
CYPRUS Tourism Cotton
LEBANON SYRIA
Beirut Poultry
Haifa Damascus
ISRAEL Tel Aviv
Jerusalem Amman
Dome of the Rock JORDAN
SIGNAI DESERT Aqaba Olives
GULF OF SUEZ Tomatoes
HEJAZ Date palm
EGYPT Cargo ship
NEJD
Petrochemical industry Grapes Tourism
Yanbu Medina
Red Sea
Shrimps
Cruise liner
ASIR Fishing industry
Scuba diving
Iron ore
Jiddah Mecca Mecca
Bedouin man SAUDI ARABIA AD DAHNA
Wolf Riyadh
Gold Bedouin tent house
ARABIAN DESERT
YEMEN
Wheat Sana Textile industry
Aden

Goats
Tobacco
LAKE VAN
Mt ARARAT 5,165 m
Tabriz
Oil
ELBUR
Natural gas
Tehran
Livestock Caviar
EUPHRATES
Hydroelectric dam Mosul
Barley Tea LAKE NAMAK Cotton
Bakhtaran GREAT SALT D
Carpets Baghdad
Timber Esfahan
Wolf IRAQ Petrochemical industry Citr
Arabian horse Ahvaz
TIGRIS Oil ZAGROS MTS Sheep
Arabian camels Abadan
Basra Shiraz
Wheat Kuwait Towers Kuwait
AN NAFUD KUWAIT Tourism
Hyena PERSIAN GULF
Oil Al Jubayl
Petrochemical industry BAHRAIN
Hyena Manama QATAR
Oil Doha
Arabian oryx U.A.
Fox Natural gas
Arabian camels RUB AL KHALI
Hydroelectric dam Potatoes Petrochemical industry
Oil Barley
Dates Oil
HADHRAMAUT
Cargo ship

N

0 200 400 600 800 Kilometres
0 100 200 300 400 500 Miles

MAN-MADE LANDMARK

Hagia Sophia, or the Church of Divine Wisdom, in Istanbul is over 1,400 years old. For 900 years it was used as a church, and as a mosque for another 500 years. This beautiful building, lined with carved and painted tiles, is now a museum.

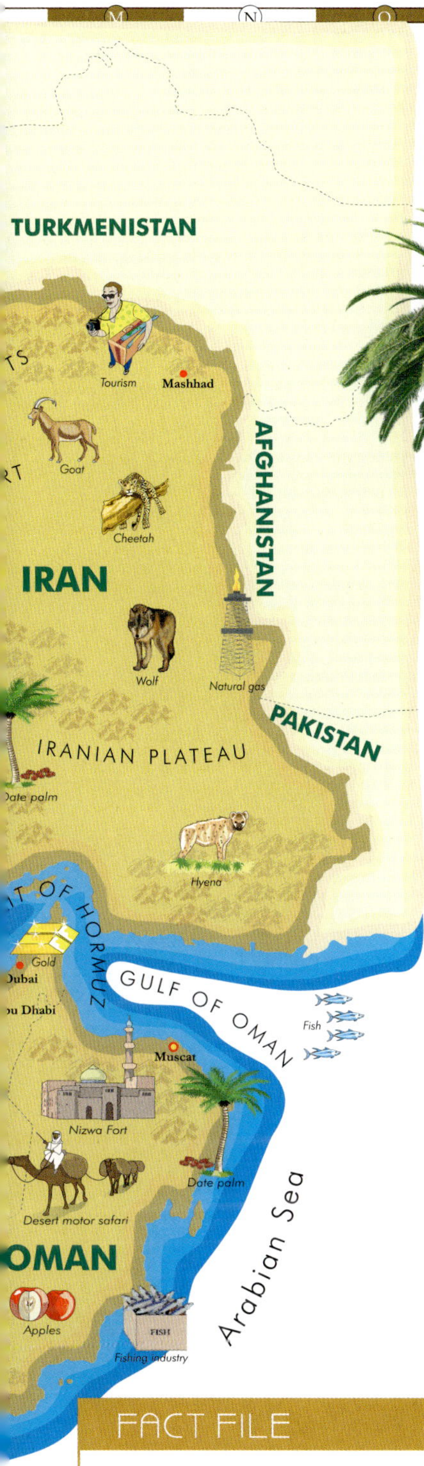

Map labels (left panel)

TURKMENISTAN

Tourism · **Mashhad**

AFGHANISTAN

Goat

Cheetah

IRAN

Wolf

Natural gas

PAKISTAN

IRANIAN PLATEAU

Date palm

...TS

...RT

Hyena

...T OF HORMUZ

Gold

...Dubai

...ou Dhabi

GULF OF OMAN

Fish

Muscat

Nizwa Fort

Desert motor safari

Date palm

OMAN

Apples

FISH

Fishing industry

Arabian Sea

FLORA AND FAUNA

The Arabian leopard, the biggest cat of the Arabian Peninsula, is found mostly in the Dhofar region in Oman. Very few survive as most have been hunted. It is lighter in colour than the African and Asian leopards.

The date palm tree grows in the oases in the dry Arabian region. The tree has large, feathery leaves and sweet, brown fruits, called dates; each has a hard seed. The date is an important food for the Arabs.

FESTIVALS AND FAIRS

Most countries in southwest Asia are Islamic. Eid-ul-Fitr is celebrated at the end of the holy month of Ramadan. People fast for the whole month, then on Eid, they feast on delicacies, visit friends and exchange presents.

FACT FILE

REPUBLIC OF TURKEY
Capital: Ankara

REPUBLIC OF CYPRUS
Capital: Nicosia

SYRIAN ARAB REPUBLIC
Capital: Damascus

REPUBLIC OF LEBANON
Capital: Beirut

STATE OF ISRAEL
Capital: Jerusalem

HASHEMITE KINGDOM OF JORDAN
Capital: Amman

REPUBLIC OF IRAQ
Capital: Baghdad

KINGDOM OF SAUDI ARABIA
Capital: Riyadh

REPUBLIC OF YEMEN
Capital: Sanaa

SULTANATE OF OMAN
Capital: Muscat

UNITED ARAB EMIRATES
Capital: Abu Dhabi

STATE OF QATAR
Capital: Doha

STATE OF BAHRAIN
Capital: Manama

STATE OF KUWAIT
Capital: Kuwait City

ISLAMIC REPUBLIC OF IRAN
Capital: Tehran

SOUTHERN ASIA

Seven countries make up Southern Asia. The Hindu Kush mountains, the Karakoram range and the Himalayas in the north separate the Indian sub-continent from Central Asia and China. Mount Everest, the highest peak in the world, is in the Himalayas. To the west of India lie Afghanistan and Pakistan. Towards the northeast of the region are the mountain kingdoms of Nepal and Bhutan. Bangladesh and Myanmar are to the east. Sri Lanka, an island country, lies in the Indian Ocean. The Eastern and Western Ghats lie along India's coastline. The Ganges flows down the northern Indian plains where rice, wheat, sugarcane and cotton are grown. The monsoons bring torrential rain to parts of southern Asia from May to September. The region houses a quarter of all the people on the planet. Over a billion people live in India alone. India is the second most populated country in the world.

FLORA AND FAUNA

Tea is grown on Sri Lankan slopes and in the hills of northeast India. Tender tea leaves are plucked and processed. Tea can be made in a variety of ways. Often it is made by pouring boiling water over the dried leaves.

The two-humped camel in Afghanistan is used to carry goods and people. It can go without food and water for days. It stores fat in its hump. The one-humped camel is found in the Thar Desert, in India and Pakistan.

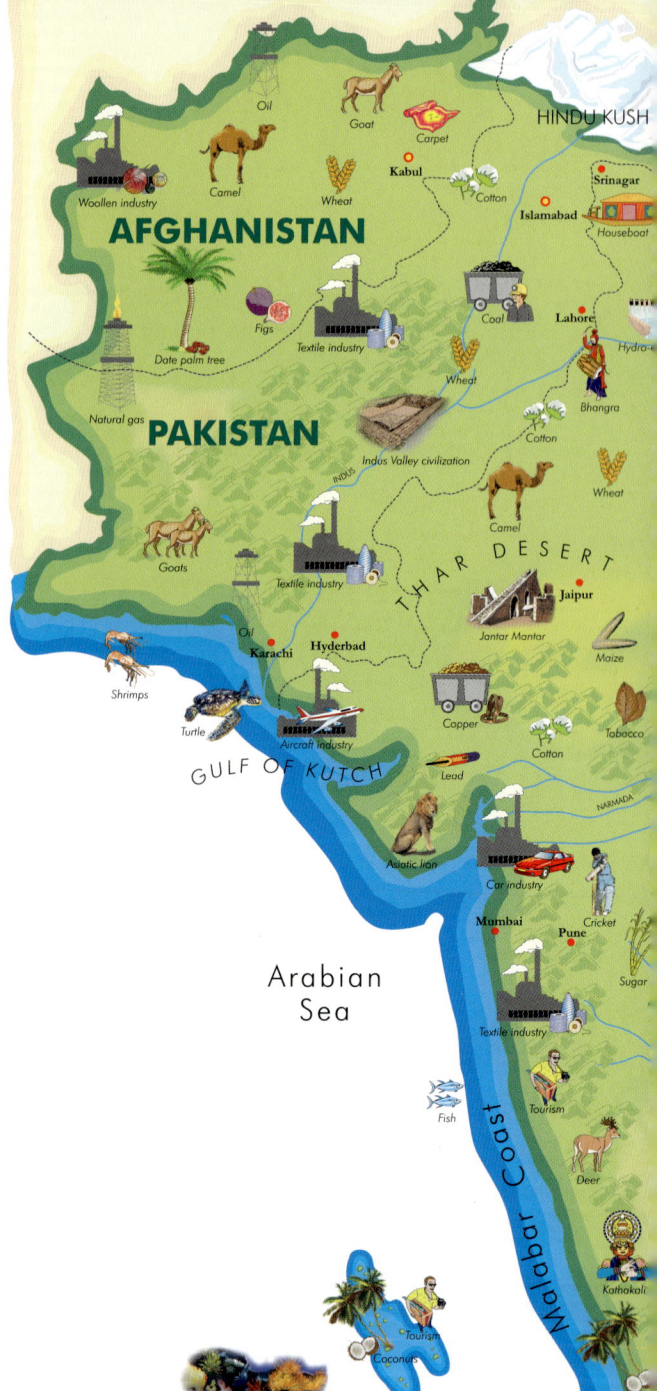

AFGHANISTAN

PAKISTAN

HINDU KUSH

Oil · Goat · Carpet
Camel · Kabul · Cotton · Srinagar
Woollen industry · Camel · Wheat · Islamabad · Houseboat

Figs · Coal · Lahore · Hydro-e
Date palm tree · Textile industry · Wheat · Bhangra
Natural gas · Cotton

Indus Valley civilization · Wheat

THAR DESERT

Goats · Camel
Textile industry · Jaipur
Jantar Mantar

Oil · Hyderbad · Maize
Karachi · Copper
Shrimps · Tobacco
Turtle · Cotton
Aircraft industry · Lead

GULF OF KUTCH

Asiatic lion · Car industry · Cricket
Mumbai · Pune
Sugar

Arabian Sea

Textile industry

Fish · Tourism

Deer

Malabar Coast

Fish · Kathakali
Coco

LAKSHADWEEP (INDIA)
Tourism
Coconuts
Coral reefs
Thiruvananthapuram

INDIAN

FESTIVALS AND FAIRS

The annual festival of Phaungdaw Oo Pagoda, held in October in the In-le lake, is full of pomp and pageantry. Images of the Buddha are taken from the pagoda and placed on the royal barge, Karaweik ('mythical bird'), which is taken around the lake.

0 200 400 600 800 Kilometres
0 100 200 300 400 500 Miles

N

CHINA

H I M A L A Y A S

Leopard

NEPAL Tourism

MT EVEREST 8,848 m

BHUTAN

Delhi

Kathmandu Thimphu

Mahai Temple

Mangoes Rhino Tea

Sitar

Taj Mahal

Agra GANGA Rice

Potatoes Elephants Bamboo Citrus fruits Timber

Diamonds

BANGLADESH

Petroleum industry

Paper industry Iron ore Victoria Memorial Hall Rice Dhaka Gemstones **BURMA** (Myanmar)

INDIA Leopard Kolkata Potatoes Mandalay

Steel industry Tiger Coconut

Coal Oil Lead

CCAN PLATEAU Rice Sun Temple

Chilli pepper Onions

Cotton GODWAR Crabs Fish Fish Rice field Maize

Hyderabad Natural gas Sugar cane

Diamonds Turtle Coral reefs Fishing trawler THILAND

Coconuts Yangon (Rangoon)

Bangalore Coconuts **Andaman Sea**

Dolphins Coconuts

Silver Chennai Shrimps

Scuba diving

Meenakshi Temple **ANDAMAN ISLANDS (INDIA)**

Rubber

SRI LANKA

Fish Elephants

Scuba diving Tea **NICOBAR ISLANDS (INDIA)**

Colombo Cricket

O C E A N Crabs Fish

Coromandel Coast

Bay of Bengal

LAOS

MAN-MADE LANDMARK

The Taj Mahal at Agra was built by the Moghul emperor Shah Jahan in the 17th century. Built of white marble, it was a tomb for his favourite wife Mumtaz Mahal, whom he loved very much. Semi-precious stones and detailed carvings decorate the stunning building.

69

FACT FILE

AFGHANISTAN
Capital: Kabul
Currency: Afghani
Population: 38,928,341
Area: 647,500 square kilometres
Language: Dari
Major Industries: Hand-woven carpets, natural gas, coal, copper

BANGLADESH
Capital: Dhaka
Currency: Taka
Population: 164,689,383
Area: 144,000 square kilometres
Language: Bangla
Major Industries: Cotton textiles, jute, garments, tea processing, paper newsprint

BHUTAN
Capital: Thimphu
Currency: Ngultrum
Population: 771,612
Area: 47,000 square kilometres
Language: Dzongkha
Major Industries: Cement, wood products, processed fruits, alcoholic beverages

MYANMAR
Capital: Naypyidaw
Currency: Kyat
Population: 54,409,794
Area: 678,500 sq km
Language: Burmese
Major Industries: Agricultural processing, woven apparel, wood and wood products, pharmaceuticals, fertilisers

INDIA
Capital: New Delhi
Currency: Indian rupee
Population: 1,398,688,366
Area: 2,973,190 square kilometres
Languages: English, Hindi
Major Industries: Textiles, chemicals, steel, cement, mining, machinery, software

NEPAL
Capital: Kathmandu
Currency: Nepalese rupee
Population: 29,136,808
Area: 140,800 square kilometres
Language: Nepali
Major Industries: Tourism, textiles, cement and brick production

PAKISTAN
Capital: Islamabad
Currency: Pakistani rupee
Population: 226,886,897
Area: 770,880 square kilometres
Language: Urdu
Major Industries: Beverages, construction materials, clothing, paper products

SRI LANKA
Capital: Sri Jayewardenepura Kotte
Currency: Sri Lankan rupee
Population: 21,919,000
Area: 65,610 square kilometres
Language: Sinhala
Major Industries: Rubber processing, tea, coconuts, tobacco, textiles

CHINA & NORTHEAST ASIA

China is the third largest country in the world. It is also the most populous. The country has two major deserts - the Taklimakan Desert located in Ugyur region and the Gobi Desert that stretches across China and Mongolia. High mountains create natural barriers in the southwest. Along the coast lies the Yellow Sea and the East and South China seas. The Yangtse River flows from the Tibetan highlands to the East China Sea. Intensive farming is practised along the river valleys. China has many modern industries. Its machinery, textile and household goods are exported all over the world. Tea, rice, maize, cotton and soybeans are grown. This big country has plenty of oil, coal, tungsten, timber and hydroelectric power. Shanghai is a big industrial city and Hong Kong is a wealthy financial centre. The island of Taiwan lies southwards, between the East and South China seas. It manufactures and exports clothing and electronic items all over the world.

FESTIVALS AND FAIRS

In late January or early February, according to the lunar calendar, the Chinese celebrate the Spring Festival, or the Chinese New Year. Houses are cleaned, new clothes bought, debts repaid and haircuts are given. The dragon dance and the lion dance are performed in the celebrations.

Map labels

RUSSIAN

KAZAKHSTAN

KYRGYZSTAN

TAJIKISTAN

AFGHANISTAN

INDIA

NEPAL

ALTAI MTS
Elk
LAKE HAR US
Camels
Coal
Potatoes
Petroleum industry
TIEN SHAN MTS
Urumqi
Steel industry
Camel riding
Coal
Kuqa
Silver
Camels
Donkey
Yumen
五羅影
梅興俠
泳贸侠
Chinese calligraphy
Kashgar (Kashi)
Woollen industry
Coal
Potatoes
Shache
Yecheng
TAKLI MAKAN DESERT
Cattle
Donkey
KUNLUN SHAN MTS
Sheep
Gold
Copper
TIBETAN PLATEAU
TIBET
Textile industry
Barley
Goat
Timber
Tiger
Giant panda
Gold
Woollen industry
Potatoes
Crane
Lhasa
BRAHMAPUTRA
YANGTSE
Tobacco
H
I
M
A
L
A
Y
A
S
MEKONG
Cattle
Timber

Scale
0 — 250 — 500 — 750 — 1000 Kilometres
0 — 150 — 300 — 450 — 600 Miles

FLORA AND FAUNA

Flora-Star Anise, with its licorice-like flavour, is a spice in the shape of an eight-pointed star. It is the fruit of a small evergreen tree. This tree bears fruit continuously for a 100 years.

The endangered Giant Panda lives in the mountainous bamboo forest. It eats bamboo shoots and leaves. The Chinese have begun a programme to save the panda. It is found in the Sichuan, Gansu and Shaanxi provinces.

MAN-MADE LANDMARK

The Great Wall of China was built by the Qin emperor in 221 B.C. The wall was built to keep out enemies from the north. Since then, the wall has been rebuilt many times.

FACT FILE

N

FEDERATION

Wheat

LAKE HULUN

Oil

Timber

Potatoes

SONGHUA

Copper

Qiqihar

Oil

Harbin

Coal

Jilin

Chemical industry

Ulan Bator

Natural gas

Horse

MONGOLIA

Wheat

Changchun

Sheep

INNER MONGOLIA

Oil

LIAO

Oil

Fushun

Mongolian Ger

Musk deer

Steel industry

Shenyang

Soya beans

GOBI DESERT

Wheat

Anshan

Crane

Baotou

Forbidden City

Dalian (Luda)

Fish

Wheat

HWANG HO

Skiing

Beijing (Peking)

Yinchuan

Reindeer

Tianjin

Sea of Japan

CHINA

Taiyuan

Livestock

YELLOW RIVER

Jinan

Oil

Carrots

Qingdao

Fish

Lanzhou

Iron ore

Tobacco

Tea

Luoyang

Zhengzhou

Soya beans

Xi'an

Oil

Cotton

Citrus fruits

Yunxian

Nanjing

YANGTZE

Jin Mao Tower

Yellow Sea

Barley

Pears

Steel industry

Shanghai

Chengdu

YANGTZE

Hangzhou

East China Sea

Rye

Nanxian

Silk industry

Nanchang

Car industry

Cotton

Tea

Wenzhou

Chongqing

Changsha

Nanping

Citrus fruits

Sugar cane

Fuzhou

Pagoda

Chinese Taipei

Guiyang

Moon cake

Kunming

Steel industry

Textile industry

Electronics

Copper

Liuzhou

Electronics

Shantou

Grass skiing

Rice

Sugar cane

Paper industry

Canton

Chaoyang

Philippine Sea

Malipo

Nanning

Rice

Hong Kong

Casino

Fishing industry

Oil rig

MACAU

VIETNAM

Coconuts

HAINAN

Fishing trawler

South China Sea

OS

Shrimp

CHINA
Capital: Beijing
Population: 1,447,131,158
Languages: Standard Chinese or Mandarin
Currency: Yuan
Area: 9,424,702.9 square kilometres

Major Industries: Iron and steel, coal, machine building, armaments, textiles and apparel, petroleum, cement, chemical fertilisers, footwear, toys, food processing, automobiles, consumer electronics, telecommunications

MONGOLIA
Capital: Ulaanbaatar
Population: 3,278,292
Language: Khalkha Mongol
Currency: Togrog/Tugrik
Area: 1.565 million square kilometres
Major Industries: Construction materials, mining, oil, food and beverages, processing of animal products

NORTH & SOUTH KOREA & JAPAN

Japan or Nippon is a chain of islands strung along the Pacific coast of eastern Asia. Some islands are peaks of submerged volcanoes, of which some are active. Mt Fuji, the highest peak is a volcano. Most of the land is mountainous and earthquakes are common. Most people live in the coastal plains, in large modern cities like Tokyo, Yokohama and Osaka. The north has a cooler climate than the south. Japan leads the world in building cars, electronics, machines and shipbuilding. However, Japan has limited natural resources. Japan has been ruled by emperors since 660

FLORA AND FAUNA

Mugunghwa, which means the 'flower of eternity', is the national flower of South Korea. It is a variety of hibiscus and is sometimes known as the Rose of Sharon. This flower stands for eternal prosperity.

The Tancho or the Japanese crane is a majestic and elegant bird. It has black and white plumage and a red spot on the head. These cranes can be seen in the Kushiro Shitsugen National Park. The Japanese believe that cranes live to be a thousand years old.

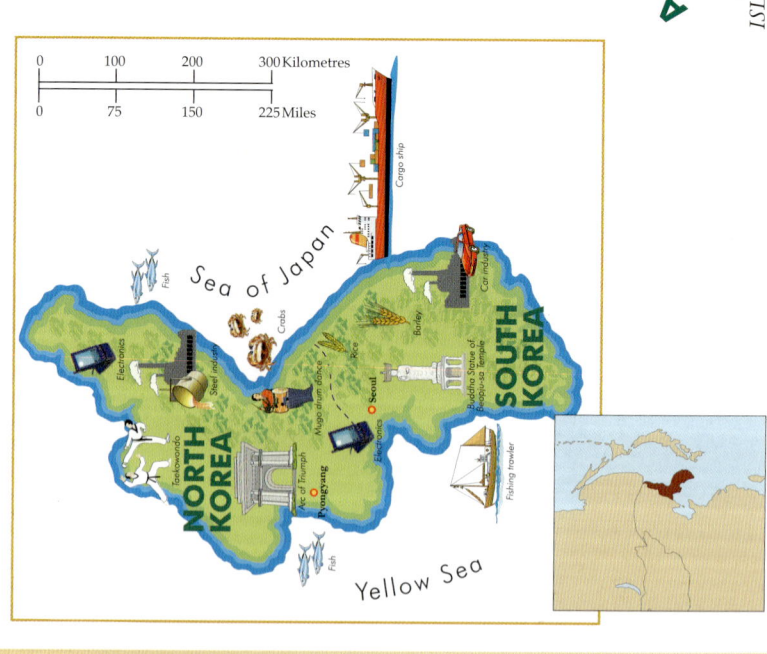

PACIFIC OCEAN

Sea of Okhotsk

Sea of Japan

Yellow Sea

KURILE ISLANDS

HOKKAIDO

HONSHU

SADO ISLANDS

OKI ISLANDS

NORTH KOREA

SOUTH KOREA

Map labels — Japan

Nemuro · Kushiro · Karate · Whale · Geyser · Japanese crane · Sapporo · Cycling · Skiing · Coal · Daisy · Japanese fan · Shrimps · Hakodate · Fishing trawler · Aomori · Apples · Morioka · Akita · Petrochemical industry · Japanese meal · Rice · Sendai · Sake (Rice wine) · Cherries · Surfing · Electronics · Petrochemical industry · Bullet train · Tokyo · Kawasaki · Yokohama · Shizuoka · Japanese drum · Salamander · Monkey · Rice · Mt FUJIYAMA 3,776 m · Car industry · Silk industry · Golf · Toyama · Ikebana flower arrangement · Japanese fan · Dolphins · Octopus · Crabs · Fish

Map labels — Korea

Sea of Japan · Fish · Crabs · Electronics · Seoul industry · Barley · Rice · Seoul · Buddha Statue of Sokkuram Temple · SOUTH KOREA · Tonkwando · Mugo drum dance · Electronics · Arc of Triumph · Pyongyang · NORTH KOREA · Fishing trawler · Cargo ship · Car industry · Fish

Scale:
0 100 200 300 Kilometres
0 75 150 225 Miles

N

FESTIVALS AND FAIRS

In South Korea on Buddha's birthday devout Buddhists hang coloured lotus lanterns. Many people write and say prayers. For the annual Lantern Parade, thousands of people walk down Seoul's streets after dark carrying lanterns, many of which they make themselves.

MAN-MADE LANDMARK

The Shinto shrine, Heian Jingu, was built in 1895 to mark Kyoto's 1,100th anniversary. Kyoto was the ancient capital of Japan. The vermillion buildings with green roofs have a garden at the back with cherry and maple trees, flowers like azaleas, iris and water lilies.

B.C. The Japanese are skilled at pottery, silk textiles, painting and architecture.

The Korean Peninsula lies to the west of Japan. This is split into two countries, North Korea and South Korea. South Korea is known for its computer and electronics industries.

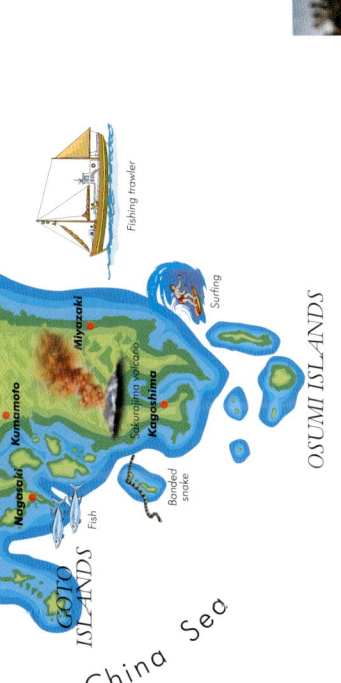

FACT FILE

JAPAN

Capital: Tokyo
Population: 125,836,021
Language: Japanese
Currency: Yen
Area: 377,835 square kilometres
Major Industries: Motor vehicles, electronic equipment, machine tools, steel and nonferrous metals, ships, chemicals, textiles, processed foods

NORTH KOREA

Capital: Pyongyang
Population: 25,778,815
Language: Korean
Currency: North Korean won
Area: 120,540 square kilometres
Major Industries: Military products; machine building, electric power chemicals; mining, metallurgy; textiles; food processing; tourism

SOUTH KOREA

Capital: Seoul
Population: 51,780,579
Language: Korean
Currency: South Korean won
Area: 98,480 square kilometres
Major Industries: Electronics, automobile production, chemicals, shipbuilding, steel, textiles, clothing, footwear, food processing

Map labels

IZU ISLANDS

Tea ceremony
Dairy
Whale
Kobe cattle
Kyoto
Textile industry
Osaka
Buddha Statue at Todaiji Temple
Tottori
Noh Theatre Mask
Okayama
Tobacco
Kochi
Sumo wrestler
SHIKOKU
Barley
Cattle
Kimono
Hiroshima
Oil
Soya beans
KYUSHU
Miyazaki
Kumamoto
Kitakyushu
Fukuoka
Kagoshima
Sakurajima volcano
Nagasaki
Coal
Banded snake
Fish
IKI
TSUSHIMA ISLANDS
GOTO ISLANDS
Fish
Fish
Scuba diving
Dolphins
Fishing trawler
Surfing
OSUMI ISLANDS
Fishing industry
East China Sea

Scale

0 50 100 150 200 250 Miles
0 100 200 300 400 Kilometres

SOUTHEAST ASIA

Southeast Asia is the vast area that lies on either side of the Equator, between the Indian and Pacific Oceans. In the north are Thailand, Laos, Cambodia and Vietnam. Towards the south lies Malaysia and the archipelago of Indonesia, consisting of over 17,000 islands. The second largest island of Indonesia is Sumatra. Borneo and the Philippines lie eastwards. Large rivers like the Mekong and the Salween wind along the foothills, across the plains and then empty out into the sea. This area has a warm, wet climate; tidal waves and earthquakes are common. Earlier this area had dense tropical forests. These have been cut down for paddy fields and crops like rubber, pineapples, coconuts, coffee, tea and opium. Rare animals like orangutans are found in the remaining rainforests. Timber is exported. Singapore, a small but wealthy country is a centre for international business and finance.

MAN-MADE LANDMARK

Angor Wat in Cambodia was built in the 12th century by King Suryavarman as a Hindu temple. It was later dedicated to Buddhism. The temple walls have beautiful sculptures depicting events associated with Hindu gods. It is a World Heritage site.

FLORA AND FAUNA

In Indonesia's rainforest, the strange rafflesia flower grows over one metre wide and can weigh about nine kilograms. This endangered, parasitic flower takes a year to bloom and finally opens at midnight. It smells of rotten meat, so is sometimes known as the corpse-flower!

The Asian elephant is found all over southeast Asia. The elephant is a symbol of fortune in Thailand, and people pass beneath it for luck. Elephants are losing their habitat and getting fewer in number.

BURMA

LAOS

Chemical industry
Hanoi
Haiphong
RED RIVER

VIETNAM

Elephants
Gemstones
Vientiane
Coffee
Crocodile

Plain of Jars
MEKONG
CHAO PHRAYA
Rice
Pineapple
Timber
Tobacco

THAILAND

Temple of the Golden Buddha
Bangkok
Black pepper
Bamboo
Hue
Da Nang
Seals

Rice

CAMBODIA

Rice

South China Sea

Andaman Sea

Fish

Tourism

Rice

GULF OF THAILAND

Peanuts
Phnom Penh
Tobacco
Tiger
Turtle

Shrimp

Bananas
Ho Chi Minh City (Saigon)
Fish

Phuket

Rubber tree

Fishing industry

Cruise liner

Fishing trawler

Banda Aceh

Cashew nuts

Electronics
Ipoh

Oil rig

Bandar Seri Begawan

BRUNEI

Oil

INDIAN OCEAN

Tapir
Medan

Petronas Towers
Kuala Lumpur

MALAYSIA

Sarawak

Rice

Johor Baharu
Singapore

Oil

LAKE TOBA

Rhinoceros

SINGAPORE

Snorkelling

Elephants

Oil

Rubber

Sumatra

Padang

Pontianak

Borneo (Indonesia)

Rice field

Gold

Coffee
Tobacco

Fish

Elephants

Banjarmasin

Coconut trees
Bamboo

Crocodile

Fishing trawler

Java Sea

INDO

Jakarta

Canoeing

Bandung
Textile industry

Surabaya
Oil

Java
Malang

Tourism
Bali

Fish

Cocos Islands

Christmas Island

Cruise liner

FACT FILE

BRUNEI
Capital: Bandar Seri Begawan
Currency: Bruneian dollar
Population: 437,483

LAOS
Capital: Vientiane
Currency: Kip
Population: 7,275,556

SINGAPORE
Capital: Singapore
Currency: Singapore dollar
Population: 5,685,807

CAMBODIA
Capital: Phnom Penh
Currency: Riel
Population: 16,718,971

MALAYSIA
Capital: Kuala Lumpur
Currency: Ringgit
Population: 32,365,998

THAILAND
Capital: Bangkok
Currency: Baht
Population: 69,799,978

EAST TIMOR
Capital: Dili
Currency: US dollar
Population: 1,318,442

PHILIPPINES
Capital: Manila
Currency: Philippine peso
Population: 109,581,085

VIETNAM
Capital: Hanoi
Currency: Dong
Population: 97,338,583

INDONESIA
Capital: Jakarta
Currency: Indonesian rupiah
Population: 273,523,621

N

Black pepper

Coral reefs

Luzon

Manila

Coconuts

PHILIPPINES

PACIFIC OCEAN

Crabs

Rice field

Cebu

Palawan

Sulu Sea

Sugar cane

Mindanao

Zamboanga

Davao

Celebes Sea

FESTIVALS AND FAIRS

The annual kite festival in Bali is held in the breezy months of June and July. It was originally celebrated as a thanksgiving for the rice harvest. Once the kite is constructed, ritual offerings are made. Usually, a priest is invited to the ceremony to give his blessings. The colours of the kites symbolise different gods.

Crocodile

Cloves

Moluccas

Tobacco

Black pepper

Petroleum refinery

Sugar cane

Sweet potatoes   **Jayapura**

Fish

Palu

Oil

Bananas   *Irian Jaya*

Celebes

Gold

Coconuts

PAPUA NEW GUINEA

Gold

Snorkelling

Fish

Rice

Banda Sea

Ujung Pandang

N ESIA

Natural gas

Arafura Sea

EAST TIMOR

Flores

Timor   **Dili**   Coffee

Coconuts

Kupang

Timor Sea

0	300	600	900	1200 Kilometres
0	150 300	450	600	750 Miles

AUSTRALASIA

Celebes

Flor

Timo

Sea

Australasia is the smallest of all the continents, and the only island continent in the world. The mountains of the Great Dividing Range run along the east coast. In the western part there are rolling hills and scrub-lands, giving way to flat, dry deserts. The hot and dry central region is called 'The Outback' by the Australians. The Great Barrier Reef, the largest coral reef in the world, lies just off the northeastern coast.

Australia is situated below the Equator, in the Southern Hemisphere. The country has its summer in December.

The original people of Australia were the aborigines, who have lived here for 50,000 years. A British sailor, Captain Cook, arrived on the east coast in the 18th century. He named it New South Wales because he thought it resembled the south coast of Wales. The first British settlers were convicts who began their new life by farming. Most people now live in big cities like Sydney, Melbourne and Perth. The southeastern island of Tasmania has a cool, wet climate. Australia has animals and plants that are not found anywhere else in the world. Kangaroos, koalas, wombats and wallabies are just some of them.

The Pacific Islands

The Pacific Islands are a part of a vast region called Oceania, which also includes Australia and New Zealand. Some islands are coral islands, whereas others are the tops of sunken volcanoes, some of which are still active.

Perth Skyline

FACT FILE

Highest Peak: Puncak Jaya, New Guinea (4,884 metres)
Lowest Point: Lake Eyre, Australia (16 metres below sea level)
Largest Desert: Great Victoria, Australia
Highest Recorded Temperature: 123° F, in Brewarrina, Australia
Lowest Recorded Temperature: -9.4° F, in Charlotte Pass, Australia
Largest Salt Lake: Lake Eyre (when full)
Active Volcano: Mount Ngauruhoe, New Zealand.

s Sea

ADMIRALTY ISLANDS

Kiribati Island

MELANESIA

s Sea

PAPUA NEW GUINEA

SOLOMON ISLANDS

PACIFIC OCEAN

Arafura Sea

Melville Island

ARNHEM LAND

GULF OF CARPENTARIA

VICTORIA

CAPE YORK PENINSULA

GREAT BARRIER REEF

Coral Sea

BARKLY TAB.L.

FLINDERS

GREAT DIVIDING RANGE

VANUATU

FIJI ISLANDS

SA

LAKE MACKAY

MAC DONNELL RANGES

NEW CALEDONIA (FR)

TONG

LAKE AMADEUS

T VICTORIA DESERT

WARREGO

LAKE EYRE

TROPIC OF CAPRIC

LAKE TORRENS

LAKE FROME

DARLING

FLINDERS RANGES

LACHLAN

OR PLAIN

LAKE GAIRDNER

AT AUSTRALIAN BIGHT

MURRAY

Kangaroo Island

CAPE HOWE

Tasman Sea

King Island

TASMANIA

SOUTHERN CAPE

North Island

COOK STRAIT

South Island

SOUTHERN ALPS

Stewart Island

0	250	500	750	1000	1250 Kilometres	
0	150	300	450	600	750 Miles	

N

Largest Monolith: Ayers Rock, Australia

Longest Mountain Range: Great Dividing Range

Largest Coral Formation: Great Barrier Reef

Longest River: Murray-Darling Basin, Australia (3,375 kilometres)

Ayers Rock is 863 metres above sea level and covers an area of 35 kilometres

AUSTRALIA & PAPUA NEW GUINEA

The continent of Australia is the sixth largest country in the world. It is fertile and green along the coastline, where most of the big cities are situated. Inland there are vast farms where sheep and cattle are raised. The central region is dry and barren. The kangaroo and the koala bear are Australia's best-known animals. They carry their young in a pouch and are called marsupials. The original inhabitants, the Aborigines, have lived here for over 40,000 years. The first European settlers came to Australia about 350 years ago.

The tropical island of Papua New Guinea lies north of Australia. It has mountains, dense rainforests and swampy marsh lands. Fierce crocodiles live in the marshes. They are also to be found in Australia. Coconuts, coffee and rubber are grown in Papua New Guinea. A large flightless bird, the cassowary, lives here.

PAPUA NEW GUINEA

NEW BRITAIN

Coffee
Timber
Rubber tree
Gold
Port Moresby

Arafura Sea

Timor Sea

INDIAN OCEAN

Whales

Darwin
Aboriginals
ARNHEM LAND
Peanuts
Boomerang
KING LEOPOLD RANGES
Uranium
Copper
NORTHERN TE
Eucal

Broome
Diamonds
Iron ore
Tourism
GREAT SANDY DESERT
The Devil's Marbles

Dolphins
Natural gas
Port Hedland
Petroleum refinery
Uranium
Sheep
Camel
LAKE MACKAY
Possum
MACDONNELL RANGE
Diamo

Wheat
HAMERSLEY RANGE
LAKE DISAPPOINTMENT
Camel
Alice Springs

GASCOYNE
Timber
WESTERN AUSTRALIA
AUSTRALIA

Fish
Natural gas
Cattle
Sheep
GIBSON DESERT
Echidna
Kangaroo
MUSGRAVE RANGES

INDIAN OCEAN

Geraldton
Turtle
Barley
Kangaroo
Gold
GREAT VICTORIA DESERT
Dingo
Camel
SOUTH AUSTRALIA
White
Gem
LAKE

Vineyards
Kalgoorlie
Dingo
Camel
Oats
Fishing Industry

Wine
Golf
Perth
Fremantle

Dolphins
Cattle
Albany
GREAT AUSTRALIAN BIGHT
Great white sharks
SOUTHERN OCEAN

Turtle
Scuba diving

FLORA AND FAUNA

The most famous Australian tree is the eucalyptus, also known as the gum tree. The koala bear lives on these trees and eats only eucalyptus leaves. Oil from the eucalyptus tree is used in perfumes, medicines and lozenges.

The national emblem of Australia is the Koala. Its fur is soft grey and it has strong, sharp claws for climbing. Baby koalas live in the mother's pouch for seven months. Koalas smell like cough drops, because they eat sharp smelling eucalyptus leaves.

FESTIVALS AND FAIRS

Henley-on-Todd Regatta is a boat race held in the arid Alice Springs of Australia. The participants hold bottomless boats and run across the dry riverbed. If it rains on the day of the race, the race is cancelled.

FACT FILE

COMMONWEALTH OF AUSTRALIA

Capital: Canberra
Population: 25,687,041
Language: English
Currency: Australian dollar
Area: 7,692,024 square kilometres
Major industries: Minerals, mining, gold, oil, meat, wool, cereals and tourism

THE INDEPENDENT STATE OF PAPUA NEW GUINEA

Capital: Port Moresby
Population: 8,947,027
Language: English
Currency: Kina
Area: 462,840 square kilometres
Major industries: Copper, gold, silver, crude oil, palm oil, coffee
Highest peak: Mt Wilhelm (4,509 metres)

MAN-MADE LANDMARK

Sydney Opera House

The design of the free-standing, sculptural Sydney Opera House is based on the segments of an orange. This beautiful building is the centre for performing arts and is the focal point of the Sydney Harbour.

GULF OF CARPENTARIA

Cape York Peninsula

Coral Sea

GREAT BARRIER REEF

PACIFIC OCEAN

Groote Eylandt

TORY

BARKLY TABLELAND

Bananas

Tourism

Cairns

Copper

Timber

Townsville

Mount Isa

Kangaroo

Uranium

Eucalyptus

Pineapples

Mackay

Sheep

Peanuts

Cotton

QUEENSLAND

Koala bear

Coal

Rockhampton

SIMPSON DESERT

Cattle

Natural gas

LAKE EYRE

Oil

Tourism

Brisbane

Southport

Wheat

Citrus fruits

LAKE TORRENS

Livestock

Woollen industry

Corn

Steel industry

Woomera

Port Augusta

DARLING

Broken Hill

NEW SOUTH WALES

GREAT DIVIDING RANGE

FLINDERS RANGES

Cotton

Industry

Tobacco

Wombat

Sydney Opera House

Mildura

MURRUMBIDGEE

Parliament House

Sydney

Adelaide

MURRAY

Wagga Wagga

Wollongong

Wine

Citrus fruits

Canberra

Tourism

VICTORIA

Albury

Windsurfing

Formula one car racing

Bendigo

Ballarat

Melbourne

Geelong

Cargo ship

BASS STRAIT

Fish

Possum

Apples

TASMANIA

Hobart

Vineyards

GREAT DIVIDING RANGE

Emperor angelfish

Coral reefs

Platypus

Wreckfish

Chocolate clownfish

Yatching

Tasman Sea

Emperor angelfish

| 0 | 200 | 400 | 600 | 800 | 1000 Kilometres |

| 0 | 150 | 300 | 450 | 600 Miles |

NEW ZEALAND

New Zealand, popularly known as Kiwiland, lies about 1,600 kilometres southeast of Australia. The lush green countryside has large pastures for sheep and cattle. With more sheep than people, New Zealand is one of the largest exporters of meat, milk and wool. The original inhabitants, the Maoris, had named the country Aotearoa, meaning 'Land of the Long White Cloud'. The country has two main islands – the North and South islands, along with a few smaller ones. Most people live on the North Island. It has sandy beaches, active volcanoes, mineral-rich hot springs, boiling mud pools and hissing geysers. The snow-capped Southern Alps run almost the entire length of South Island. Huge glaciers have carved out deep fjords into the coast. The fast-moving rivers in the country are used to generate hydroelectricity.

MAN-MADE LANDMARK

The 'City of Sails', Auckland, is a retreat for sea adventurers. Completely surrounded by water, it is the country's largest city and port. The Sky Tower, also in Auckland, is the tallest building in the southern hemisphere.

Map labels

PACIFIC OCEAN

N

NEW ZEALAND

Tasman Sea

North Island

Pine trees
Fish
Timber
Oil
Whangarei
Snorkelling
Geyser
Paper industry
Auckland
Sky Tower
Yachting
BAY OF PLENTY
Windsurfing
Tramping
Hamilton
Tauranga
Rotorua
Geyser
Paragliding
Dairy
Avocados
Oil
LAKE TAUPO
Maori Poi dance
Citrus fruits
Gisborne
New Plymouth
Apples
Strawberries
Mt TARANAKI (Mt EGMONT) 2,518 m
Cheese
Sheep
Napier
Wanganui
Hastings
HAWKE BAY
Natural gas
Cattle
Wine
Wellington
TASMAN BAY
COOK STRAIT
The Beehive
Kiwi fruits
Nelson
Wine
Blenheim
Apples
Coal
Greymouth
Nguru
Tukutuku
Kaikoura
Kiwi
Cricket
Seals
AORAKI Mt COOK 3,764 m
Skiing
Sheep
Christchurch
CANTERBURY PLAINS
Sea lion
Hang gliding
Timaru
SOUTHERN ALPS
Sea lion
Sutherland Falls
White water rafting
Bungee jumping
Kayaking
Rugby
Yellow-eyed penguin
Woollen industry
Dunedin
Kakapo
Royal albatross
Invercargill
Coal
FOVEAUX STRAIT
Lobsters
Dolphins
Shark
Parakeet
Catlins Forest
Stewart Island
South Island
Tasman Sea
PACIFIC OCEAN

Scale

```
0    100    200    300    400 Kilometres
0   50   100   150   200   250 Miles
```

FESTIVALS AND FAIRS

Farmers from all over New Zealand take part in the Golden Shears Sheep-Shearing Contest, held every March in Masterton. The farmer who shears the wool off the sheep at the earliest is the winner. Over 700 sheep may be shorn in a single round!

FLORA AND FAUNA

New Zealand is home to flightless birds, such as the kiwi, the kakapo, the weka, or the 'mighty moa'! While the moa is believed to be extinct, the kiwi is found only in New Zealand. The only bird with nostrils at the end of the beak, the kiwi is also the country's national emblem.

Oranges, lemons, grapefruit, and apples grow in the country. The juicy kiwi fruit was first brought from China about a hundred years ago.

FACT FILE

NEW ZEALAND

Capital: Wellington
Population: 5,084,300
Languages: English and Maori
Currency: New Zealand dollar
Area: 268,680 square kilometres
Major industries: Wool, dairy and timber products, food processing
Highest Peak: Mt Cook, or Aoraki, 'Cloud Piercer', (3,754 metres)
Longest River: Waikato River (425 kilometres)
Largest Glacier: Tasman Glacier

FLAGS
OF THE
WORLD

FLAGS
THROUGH TIME

Chinese flag

Indian *dhvaja*

Islamic flag

Cross of St George

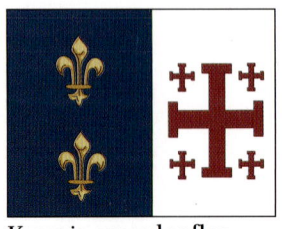
Kyrenia crusader flag

In ancient times, it was the flag that told one if the approaching individual was a friend or foe. The flag also helped a discouraged army to renew the fight with spirit.

Those battle flags were first devised by the Chinese and the Indians. It is believed that, as far back as 1122 bc, the founder of China's Chou Dynasty travelled with a white-coloured flag as his emblem. The royal flag was identified with the prestige of the king's office and it was considered a crime to show it any disrespect. The fall of the flag would signify defeat for the king and, hence, its protection was entrusted to an able general. Standard motifs in Chinese flags included the blue dragon, the red bird and the white tiger.

Indian flags commonly featured a figure designed in golden shades and fringe, against a scarlet or green background. The shape was often triangular. The flags were usually mounted on chariots or elephants, especially during a battle.

In contrast, Islamic flags were one plain colour – black, white, or red. This was because Islam disallowed the usage of any known image. Over the course of time green, which was the colour of the 10th-century-AD Fatimid Dynasty, was adopted by Islam.

Europe took its own time to embrace the idea of the flag. In the Middle Ages, leaders began using the flag of their patron saint to represent their country – for instance, the Cross of St George (white with a red cross) was widely used in 13th-century England. The oldest European flags still in use are those with the Christian cross, which was widely used in the Crusades – military wars fought against Muslims in the 11th–13th centuries.

By the end of the Middle Ages, flags became the standard symbols of nations, cities, organisations and guilds. They also began to find uses for signalling and for decoration and display. Special meanings came to be associated with particular types and colours of flags. The white flag has been used as a universal signal for peace. Similarly, the black flag became the symbol of pirates and, later, of mourning.

Over time, nations adopted flags to represent themselves. The colours and designs of these flags go back a long time – to the history, culture, values and struggles of a particular country and era.

The study of the various aspects of flags is known as vexillology (from the Latin *vexillum*, meaning 'banner'). Some sources assert it was the Roman Empire's *vexillum* that was the first 'true' flag.

Roman *vexillum*

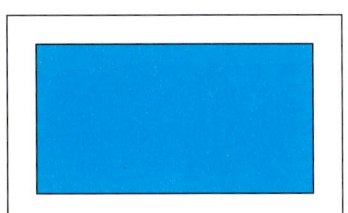
Border

Bicolour

Tricolour

Quartered

Cross

Scandinavian Cross

Saltire

Couped Cross

TYPES OF FLAGS

The colours in a flag follow a 'fixed and ordered pattern', and certainly cannot be altered as and when one wishes. A flag's colours usually have a history behind their adoption and bear distinct meanings. Flags are usually rectangular, though one sees flags in squares, pennants, swallowtails and other shapes too. The flag of Nepal is, in fact, a combination of two triangular forms!

Typically, designs on flags are crosses, stripes, stars and divisions of the surface (field) into bands. Flags are mainly distinguished by their respective national symbols. Flags may also feature different designs on each side, as can be seen on several flags of the U.S. states.

Triangle

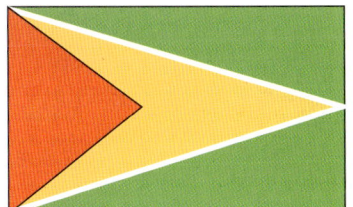
Fimbriation

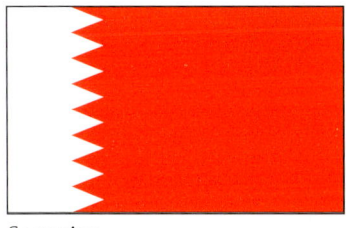
Serration

NORTH AND CENTRAL
AMERICA

Canada, the second largest country in the world, takes up nearly two-fifths of the North American continent. Canada and the United States share a border about 8,895 kilometres (5,527 miles) long. Another country sharing a common border with the United States is Mexico. The world's largest island, Greenland, lies in the North Atlantic Ocean. Two-thirds of the island falls within the Arctic Circle and over 80 per cent of the surface is ice-capped.

BELIZE

Adopted on: September 21, 1981
Ratio: 3:5
Capital: Belmopan
Independence from the United Kingdom: September 21, 1981
What it means: The blue is the colour of the main political party, People's United Party (PUP), while the red represents the opposition United Democratic Party (UDP). The national coat of arms is featured in the middle.

CANADA

Adopted on: February 15, 1965
Ratio: 1:2
Capital: Ottawa
Independence (union of British North American colonies): July 1, 1867
What it means: Red and white are the national colours of Canada. The maple leaf at the centre is a national symbol.

COSTA RICA

Adopted on: September 29, 1848
Ratio: 3:5
Capital: San Jose
Independence from Spain: September 15, 1821
What it means: Blue and white are the original colours used by the United Provinces of Central America. The red, white and blue at the bottom are inspired by the French tricolour.

EL SALVADOR

Adopted on: May 17, 1912
Ratio: 4:7
Capital: San Salvador
Independence from Spain: September 15, 1821
What it means: Blue and white are the original colours used by the United Provinces of Central America. The coat of arms includes the national motto "God, union, liberty".

GREENLAND

Adopted on: June 21, 1985
Ratio: 2:3
Capital: Nuuk (Godthab)
Independence: none; self-governing part of the Kingdom of Denmark
What it means: The white stands for the island's ice cap and glaciers, while the red is symbolic of the fjords and the sun.

GUATEMALA

Adopted on: August 17, 1871
Ratio: 5:8
Capital: Guatemala
Independence from Spain: September 15, 1821
What it means: Blue and white are the original colours used by the United Provinces of Central America. The coat of arms features the national bird, the quetzal, as a symbol of liberty.

HONDURAS

Adopted on: February 16, 1866
Ratio: 1:2
Capital: Tegucigalpa
Independence from Spain: September 15, 1821
What it means: The colours and the five stars represent the United Provinces of Central America.

MEXICO

Adopted on: November 2, 1821
Ratio: 4:7
Capital: Mexico City
Independence from Spain: September 16, 1810
What it means: The colours are those of the national liberation army of Mexico. The coat of arms features the badge of Mexico City.

GREENLAND

Nuuk
(Godthab) ⊙

CANADA

Ottawa ⊙

Washington, D.C. ⊙

UNITED STATES OF AMERICA

MEXICO

Mexico City ⊙

Belmopan
Guatemala

BELIZE

Tegucigalpa

HONDURAS

GUATEMALA ⊙

NICARAGUA

San Salvador

Managua

EL SALVADOR

PANAMA

San Jose

COSTA RICA

Panama
City

NICARAGUA

Adopted on: September 4, 1908
Ratio: 3:5
Capital: Managua
Independence from Spain: September 15, 1821
What it means: The flag features the original colours used by the United Provinces of Central America. The five volcanoes in the coat of arms represent the five original Central American countries.

PANAMA

Adopted on: November 3, 1903
Ratio: 2:3
Capital: Panama City
Independence from Colombia: November 3, 1903; from Spain on November 28, 1821
What it means: Modelled on the U.S. flag, the red and blue originally represented the Liberal and Conservative parties, respectively. White symbolises peace.

UNITED STATES OF AMERICA

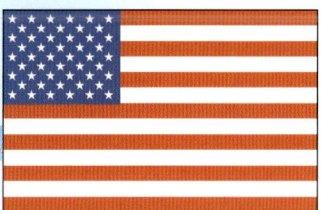

Adopted on: July 4, 1960
Ratio: 10:19
Capital: Washington, D.C.
Independence from Great Britain: July 4, 1776
What it means: The 50 stars represent the 50 states of the Union, while the 13 stripes stand for the 13 original states.

SOUTH
AMERICA

Located between the Pacific and Atlantic oceans, the continent of South America is roughly triangular in shape. It is the fourth largest continent. Mount Aconcagua in Argentina is the continent's highest point. Argentina also boasts the continent's lowest point – the Valdés Peninsula.

GUYANA

Georgetown

Caracas

SURINAME

VENEZUELA

Paramaribo

Cayenne

ECUADOR

Bogot

FRENCH GUIANA

COLOMBIA

Quito

PERU

BRAZIL

Lima

BOLIVIA

Brasilia

La Paz

PARAGUAY

CHILE

Asuncion

ARGENTINA

Santiago

URUGUAY

Buenos Aires

Montevideo

FALKLAND ISLANDS

Stanley

ARGENTINA

Adopted: 1812
Ratio: 1:2 and 9:14 on land; 2:3 at sea
Capital: Buenos Aires
Independence from Spain: July 9, 1816
What it means: The 'Sun of May' emblem refers to the events of May 1810, when, just before a battle, General Belgrano, who designed the flag, looked up and saw the clouds part to show the blue sky and the shining sun.

BOLIVIA

Adopted: 1851
Ratio: 2:3
Capital: La Paz
Independence from Spain: August 6, 1825
What it means: Red is said to represent valour, yellow the country's mineral wealth, and green the fertile land.

BRAZIL

Adopted: 1889
Ratio: 7:10
Capital: Brasilia
Independence from Portugal:
September 7, 1822
What it means: The green field is a symbol for Brazil's forests, while the yellow diamond represents gold. The blue disc features the motto 'Order and progress'.

CHILE

Adopted: 1817
Ratio: 2:3
Capital: Santiago
Independence from Spain:
September 18, 1810
What it means: Blue is symbolic of the sky; white stands for the snow on the Andes Mountains; and red recalls the blood that was shed in the long freedom struggle.

COLOMBIA

Adopted: 1819
Ratio: 2:3
Capital: Bogotá
Independence from Spain:
July 20, 1810
What it means: Yellow is said to be symbolic of sovereignty and justice, blue of loyalty, and red of courage.

ECUADOR

Adopted: 1860
Ratio: 1:2
Capital: Quito
Independence from Spain:
May 24, 1822
What it means: The colours are those of the tricolour flown by the South American revolutionary Francisco de Miranda.

FALKLAND ISLANDS

Adopted: 1948
Ratio: 1:2
Capital: Stanley
Independence: None; self-governing territory of the United Kingdom
What it means: The ram featured in the national coat of arms represents the islands' sheep industry. The U.K. flag is incorporated on the hoist side.

FRENCH GUIANA

Adopted: --
Ratio: 2:3
Capital: Cayenne
Independence: None; overseas department of France
What it means: Uses the flag of France.

GUYANA

Adopted: 1966
Ratio: 3:5 on land; 1:2 at sea
Capital: Georgetown
Independence from the United Kingdom: May 26, 1966
What it means: The yellow triangle symbolises a bright future; red, the people's zeal in building the nation; and black, determination.

PARAGUAY

Adopted: 1842
Ratio: 3:5
Capital: Asuncion
Independence from Spain:
May 14, 1811
What it means: The coat of arms depict the 'Star of May', a symbol of freedom. The treasury seal on the other side has the motto 'Peace and justice'.

PERU

Adopted: 1825
Ratio: 2:3
Capital: Lima
Independence from Spain:
July 28, 1821
What it means: Red and white are associated with the ancient Inca people, who ruled Peru for centuries. The coat of arms is featured only when the government uses the flag.

SURINAME

Adopted: 1975
Ratio: 2:3
Capital: Paramaribo
Independence from the Netherlands:
November 25, 1975
What it means: The green stripes are symbolic of the country's forests; white of justice and freedom; and red of the spirit of a new nation. The star represents unity and hope.

URUGUAY

Adopted: 1830
Ratio: 2:3
Capital: Montevideo
Independence from Brazil:
August 25, 1825
What it means: The nine stripes are for the nine original departments of the republic. Like several other South American countries, the Uruguay flag features the 'Sun of May'.

VENEZUELA

Adopted: 1836
Ratio: 2:3
Capital: Caracas
Independence from Spain:
July 5, 1811
What it means: The arc of seven stars represents the original seven provinces that supported the independence movement.

THE
CARIBBEAN

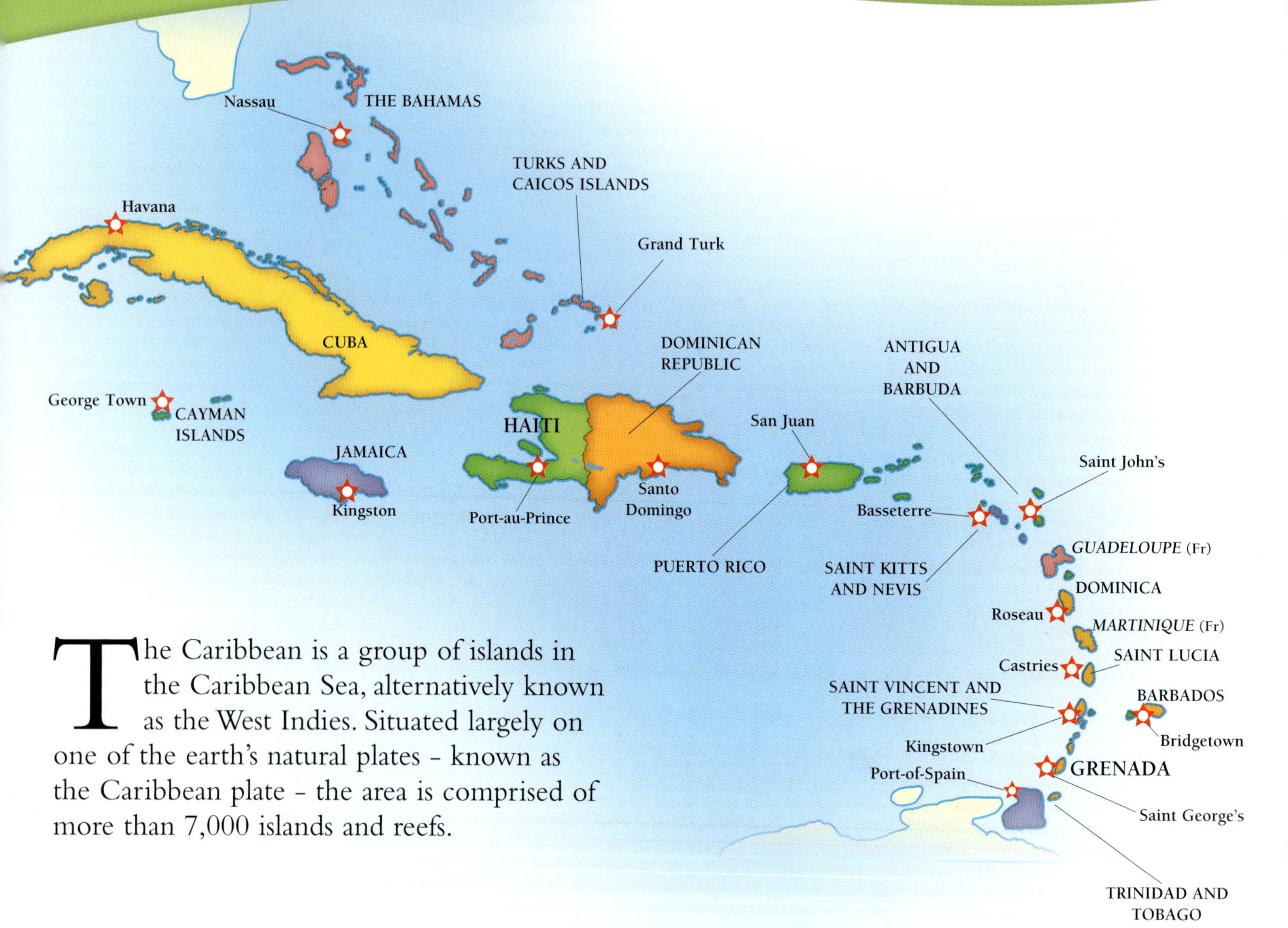

Nassau

THE BAHAMAS

TURKS AND
CAICOS ISLANDS

Grand Turk

Havana

CUBA

DOMINICAN
REPUBLIC

ANTIGUA
AND
BARBUDA

George Town

CAYMAN
ISLANDS

San Juan

Saint John's

JAMAICA

HAITI

Santo
Domingo

Basseterre

GUADELOUPE (Fr)

Kingston

Port-au-Prince

PUERTO RICO

SAINT KITTS
AND NEVIS

DOMINICA

Roseau

MARTINIQUE (Fr)

Castries

SAINT LUCIA

SAINT VINCENT AND
THE GRENADINES

BARBADOS

Bridgetown

Kingstown

Port-of-Spain

GRENADA

Saint George's

TRINIDAD AND
TOBAGO

The Caribbean is a group of islands in the Caribbean Sea, alternatively known as the West Indies. Situated largely on one of the earth's natural plates – known as the Caribbean plate – the area is comprised of more than 7,000 islands and reefs.

ANTIGUA AND BARBUDA

Adopted: 1967
Ratio: About 2:3
Capital: Saint John's
Independence from the United Kingdom: November 1, 1981
What it means: The V shape in the centre stands for victory, while the sun symbolises the dawn of a new era.

THE BAHAMAS

Adopted: 1973
Ratio: 1:2
Capital: Nassau
Independence from the United Kingdom: July 10, 1973
What it means: The aquamarine stripes are for the waters around the islands; the yellow for the sandy beaches; and the black triangle for the strength of the people.

BARBADOS

Adopted: 1966
Ratio: 2:3
Capital: Bridgetown
Independence from the United Kingdom: November 30, 1966
What it means: The blue-yellow-blue stripes stand for sea, sand and sky. The trident head is symbolic of the nation's break from its colonial history.

CAYMAN ISLANDS

Adopted: 1959
Ratio: 1:2
Capital: George Town
Independence: None; overseas territory of the United Kingdom
What it means: The three stars in the coat of arms represent the three main islands, while the pineapple and the turtle stand for the flora and fauna.

CUBA

Adopted: 1902
Ratio: 1:2
Capital: Havana
Independence from Spain: December 10, 1898
What it means: The red triangle is said to be a symbol for equality, and the white star in it stands for independence.

DOMINICA

Adopted: 1978
Ratio: 1:2
Capital: Roseau
Independence from the United Kingdom: November 3, 1978
What it means: The yellow-white-black cross represents the island's original inhabitants. The ring of 10 stars represents the 10 parishes.

DOMINICAN REPUBLIC

Adopted: 1844
Ratio: 5:8
Capital: Santo Domingo
Independence from Haiti: February 27, 1844
What it means: The white cross represents faith. When used officially, the flag features the coat of arms bearing the flag, the Holy Bible and a cross.

GRENADA

Adopted: 1974
Ratio: 3:5
Capital: Saint George's
Independence from the United Kingdom: February 7, 1974
What it means: The outer stars represent the six parishes and the central star, the capital.

GUADELOUPE

Adopted: --
Ratio: 2:3
Capital: Basse-Terre
Independence: None; overseas department of France
What it means: The flag of France is used.

HAITI

Adopted: 1803
Ratio: 3:5
Capital: Port-au-Prince
Independence from France: January 1, 1804
What it means: The blue and red are taken from the French tricolour. The coat of arms is inscribed with the motto 'Union makes strength'.

JAMAICA

Adopted: 1962
Ratio: 1:2
Capital: Kingston
Independence from the United Kingdom: August 6, 1962
What it means: the black, yellow and green represent, respectively, the difficulties suffered by the nation, the shining sun, and the fertile land.

PUERTO RICO

Adopted: 1922
Ratio: 1:2
Capital: San Juan
Independence: None; self-governing commonwealth associated with the United States
What it means: The white stripes symbolise liberty, and the red ones and the triangle, the legislative, executive and judicial branches of the state.

SAINT KITTS AND NEVIS

Adopted: 1983
Ratio: About 2:3
Capital: Basseterre
Independence from the United Kingdom: September 19, 1983
What it means: The green triangle represents land and the red one, years of freedom struggle. The black symbolises the islands' African heritage.

SAINT LUCIA

Adopted: 1967
Ratio: 1:2
Capital: Castries
Independence from the United Kingdom: February 22, 1979
What it means: The blue is for the Caribbean Sea. The triangles are for the famous twin peaks of the Pitons.

SAINT VINCENT AND THE GRENADINES

Adopted: 1985
Ratio: 2:3
Capital: Kingstown
Independence from the United Kingdom: October 27, 1979
What it means: The green diamonds represent the 'Gems of the Antilles', as the islands are known. The V shape refers to the first alphabet in Vincent.

TRINIDAD AND TOBAGO

Adopted: 1962
Ratio: 3:5
Capital: Port-of-Spain
Independence from the United Kingdom: August 31, 1962
What it means: The white stripes symbolise the sea. Red represents the vitality of the people, and black, their strength.

WESTERN EUROPE

Western Europe is made up of a widely varying landscape – from Spain, located at the intersection of Europe and Africa, to the island nation of Iceland, which has an abundance of glaciers and geysers. The 'emerald isle' of Ireland boasts an Atlantic coastline with a 3,200-kilometre- (2,000-mile)-wide stretch of ocean.

ANDORRA

Adopted: 1866
Ratio: 2:3
Capital: Andorra la Vella
Independence: 1278
What it means: The colours are taken from the flags of France and Spain, which have joint jurisdiction over the principality. The Andorran coat of arms is featured in the centre.

BELGIUM

Adopted: 1831
Ratio: 13:15
Capital: Brussels
Independence from the Netherlands: October 4, 1830
What it means: The colours have been taken from the national coat of arms – black from the shield, gold from the lion, and red from the lion's claws and tongue.

FRANCE

Adopted: 1794
Ratio: 2:3
Capital: Paris
Independence: 843, Treaty of Verdun
What it means: The colours stand for the ideals of the 1789 French Revolution – liberty, equality and fraternity.

ICELAND

Adopted: 1915
Ratio: 18:25
Capital: Reykjavik
Independence from Denmark: June 17, 1944
What it means: The red is thought to symbolise the volcanoes in the island country. White is for snow and ice, and blue is the bordering Atlantic Ocean. The cross design is based on the Danish flag.

IRELAND (EIRE)

Adopted: 1919
Ratio: 1:2
Capital: Dublin
Independence from the United Kingdom: December 6, 1921
What it means: Green is symbolic of the Roman Catholics, orange of the Protestants, and white of peace between the two sects.

ITALY

Adopted: 1919
Ratio: 2:3
Capital: Rome
Independence (Kingdom of Italy proclaimed): March 17, 1861
What it means: One legend has it that the green in the flag was used since it was the favourite colour of Napoleon. However, the green and the white might also have been based on the uniforms of the militia of Milan, Italy.

LUXEMBOURG

Adopted: 1972
Ratio: 3:5
Capital: Luxembourg
Independence from the Netherlands: 1839
What it means: The colours go back to the 13th-century coat of arms used by the grand duke.

MALTA

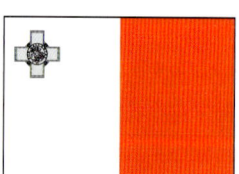

Adopted: 1964
Ratio: 2:3
Capital: Valletta
Independence from the United Kingdom: September 21, 1964
What it means: The colours were taken from the badge used by the Knights of Malta.

MONACO

Adopted: 1881
Ratio: 4:5
Capital: Monaco
Independence (the House of Grimaldi begins its rule): 1419
What it means: The red and white are the heraldic colours of the House of Grimaldi.

NETHERLANDS

Adopted: 1937
Ratio: 2:3
Capital: Amsterdam
Independence: January 23, 1579
What it means: The colours were originally taken from the livery colours of William of Orange, a Dutch prince (the orange was later replaced by red).

ICELAND
Reykjavik

PORTUGAL

Adopted: 1911
Ratio: 2:3
Capital: Lisbon
Independence (Kingdom of Portugal recognized): 1143
What it means: Green represents the Portuguese explorer, King Henry the Navigator. Red was the colour of the revolutionary flag. The central shield is symbolic of the country's history of ocean exploration.

SAN MARINO

Adopted: 1862
Ratio: 3:4
Capital: San Marino
Independence (republic founded): September 3, c. ad 301; treaty with Italy signed in 1862 recognising independence under Italy's protection
What it means: White is symbolic of the snow on Mount Titano, the country's highest point, and blue symbolises the sky.

Northern
Ireland

Scotland

EIRE
Dublin

UNITED
KINGDOM

England

Wales

NETHERLANDS
Amsterdam

London

BELGIUM

Brussels

LUXEMBOURG

Paris
Luxembourg

FRANCE

SWITZERLAND

Bern

PORTUGAL

Lisbon
Madrid

Andorra

SPAIN

ANDORRA

Monaco

MONACO

CORSICA

ITALY

SAN MARINO

San Marino

Rome

SARDINIA

VATICAN
CITY

SICILY

MALTA
Valletta

SPAIN

Adopted: 1927
Ratio: 2:3
Capital: Madrid
Independence (unification of several independent kingdoms): 1492
What it means: Red and yellow are the original colours of the coat of arms of the Castile and Aragon regions.

SWITZERLAND

Adopted: 1889
Ratio: Square in proportion
Capital: Bern
Independence (founding of the confederation): August 1, 1291
What it means: The design is based on the war flag used by the Holy Roman Empire.

UNITED KINGDOM

Adopted: 1801
Ratio: 1:2
Capital: London
Independence (current name of the United Kingdom of Great Britain and Northern Ireland adopted): 1927
What it means: The design features three crosses – of St George (England), St Andrew (Scotland) and St Patrick (Ireland).

VATICAN CITY

Adopted: 1929
Ratio: Square in proportion
Capital: Vatican City
Independence from Italy: February 11, 1929
What it means: The colours are those of the keys of St Peter's. The emblem itself features the keys upholding the papal crown.

CENTRAL EUROPE

Central Europe is a loose term applying to those countries lying between Eastern and Western Europe. One of the most recently formed of these is Slovenia. Slovenia has been shaped by limestone plateaus, ridges, caves, underground rivers, valleys and the steep Alpine peaks. There is also a short coastal strip to its southwest. The landscape of Slovakia is marked by the Western Carpathian Mountains. The Alps forms a natural and majestic barrier for the countries of Germany and Austria.

AUSTRIA

Adopted: 1945
Ratio: 2:3
Capital: Vienna
Independence (proclaimed republic):
November 12, 1918
What it means: The colours red and white have long been associated with the Austrian legend of the Battle of Acre and the blood-stained white tunic of the war hero, Luitpold V of Badenberg.

CZECHIA

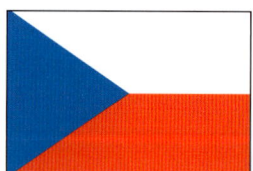

Adopted: 1920
Ratio: 2:3
Capital: Prague
Independence: January 1, 1993
(Czechoslovakia split into the Czech Republic and Slovakia)
What it means: The stripes are the herladic colours of Bohemia, which make up a large part of the Czech Republic. The blue of the isosceles triangle was used to represent the state of Moravia in the republic.

SWEDEN

FINLAND

NORWAY

Oslo

Helsinki

Stockholm

DENMARK

Copenhagen

Berlin

Warsaw

GERMANY

POLAND

Prague
CZECH
REPUBLIC

Vienna

Bratislava

Vaduz

AUSTRIA

SLOVAK REPUBLIC

LIECHTENSTEIN

Ljubljana

SLOVENIA

DENMARK

Adopted in: 1625 (oldest European flag)
Ratio: 28:34 (can be extended to 37)
Capital: Copenhagen
Independence (became a constitutional monarchy): June 5, 1849
What it means: The flag (Dannebrog) is claimed to be a token from the Pope given at the time of the Crusades. The cross design (Scandinavian Cross) was later adopted by other regional flags.

FINLAND

Adopted: 1918
Ratio: 11:18
Capital: Helsinki
Independence from Russia: December 6, 1917
What it means: The blue is for the thousands of lakes in Finland, and the white for the snow. When flown by the government, the flag has the coat of arms featuring a lion.

GERMANY

Adopted: 1949
Ratio: 3:5
Capital: Berlin
Independence (federal republic proclaimed): May 23, 1949
What it means: The colours were taken after the uniforms of German soldiers who fought in the Napoleonic Wars (1804-1815).

LIECHTENSTEIN

Adopted: 1937
Ratio: 3:5
Capital: Vaduz
Independence from the Holy Roman Empire: July 12, 1806
What it means: The crown symbolises the independence of the principality. Blue and red respectively stand for the sky and the evening fires at homes.

NORWAY

Adopted: 1821
Ratio: 8:11
Capital: Oslo
Independence (union with Sweden declared dissolved): June 7, 1905
What it means: The tricolour is a symbol of liberty, and influenced by the French, U.K. and U.S. flags. The cross takes after the design of the Danish and Swedish flags.

POLAND

Adopted: 1919
Ratio: 5:8
Capital: Warsaw
Independence: November 11, 1918
What it means: The white and red have traditionally been associated with Poland's coat of arms.

SLOVAKIA

Adopted: 1992
Ratio: 2:3
Capital: Bratislava
Independence (Czechoslovakia split into the Czech Republic and Slovakia): January 1, 1993
What it means: The flag features the traditional pan-Slavic colours.

SLOVENIA

Adopted: 1991
Ratio: 1:2
Capital: Ljubljana
Independence from Yugoslavia: June 25, 1991
What it means: The colours are the traditional pan-Slavic colours used on the flags of the Slavic peoples of Europe. The coat of arms is said to be based on the one used by the duchy of Celje.

SWEDEN

Adopted: 1906
Ratio: 5:8
Capital: Stockholm
Independence: June 6, 1523
What it means: The yellow and blue colours are those of the national coat of arms. The cross, again, is designed after the Danish flag.

EASTERN EUROPE

Geographically, Eastern Europe is marked as the region extending from the Ural and Caucasus mountains in the east to the western border of Russia. Nearly all the countries in this region gained independence only in the 20th century. Russia is the world's largest country, occupying about double the area of the United States!

ALBANIA

Adopted on: April 7, 1992
Ratio: 5:7
Capital: Tiranë
Independence from the Ottoman Empire: November 28, 1912
What it means: The double-headed black eagle represents an incident when a native prince of the 15th century successfully raised his red-coloured flag bearing the eagle, in rebellion against the Turks.

BELARUS

Adopted: 1995
Ratio: 1:2
Capital: Minsk
Independence (from Soviet Union): August 25, 1991
What it means: The red is thought to signify the blood shed by the patriots of Belarus. The red embroidered pattern is Belarusian national ornamentation.

BOSNIA AND HERZEGOVINA

Adopted: February 1998
Ratio: 1:2
Capital: Sarajevo
Independence from Yugoslavia; declared: March 3, 1992
What it means: The three points of the yellow triangle are understood to stand for the three nations of Bosnia: Bosniaks, Croats and Serbs

BULGARIA

Adopted: 1990
Ratio: 3:5
Capital: Sofia
Independence (declared; from Ottoman Empire): September 22, 1908
What it means: The white stands for peace, love and freedom; the green for the country's agricultural resources; and the red for the independence movement and the courage of the freedom fighters.

CROATIA

Adopted: 1990
Ratio: 1:2
Capital: Zagreb
Independence from Yugoslavia: June 25, 1991
What it means: The stripes feature the traditional pan-Slavic colours. The national coat of arms in the middle has a main shield with five shields on top. The checkerboard design is an ancient symbol of the Croatian kings.

ESTONIA

Adopted: 1990
Ratio: 7:11
Capital: Tallinn
Independence (recognised; from Soviet Union): August 20, 1991
What it means: The blue is a symbol of faith as well as the sky, seas and lakes; black of historic suppression as well as the soil; and white represents virtue, enlightenment and snow, as also for the country's freedom struggle.

GREECE

Adopted: 1822
Ratio: 2:3
Capital: Athens
Independence from the Ottoman Empire: 1829
What it means: The nine stripes are taken for the nine syllables in the battle cry for independence, translated as "Freedom or death". The cross symbolises Greek religious faith.

RUSSIA

KOSOVO

Adopted: February 17, 2008
Ratio: 2:3
Capital: Pristina
Independence (from Serbia, declared): February 2008
What it means: The six stars represent Kosovo's six major ethnic groups: Albanians, Serbs, Turks, Gorani, Roma and Bosniaks. The blue background is designed to be neutral.

HUNGARY

Adopted on: October 1, 1957
Ratio: 2:3
Capital: Budapest
Independence (unification by King Stephen I): 1001
What it means: Designed after the French tricolour. The red stands for strength, green for hope, and white for faithfulness.

LATVIA

Adopted: 1900
Ratio: 1:2
Capital: Riga
Independence (recognised; from Soviet Union): August 21, 1991
What it means: The flag represents a legend about a Latvian tribal leader who was wrapped in a white cloth after he was injured in a battle. A part of the cloth became stained with his blood, while the rest remained white.

LITHUANIA

Adopted: 1989
Ratio: 3:5
Capital: Vilnius
Independence (recognised; from Soviet Union): September 6, 1991
What it means: The yellow symbolises ripening wheat and freedom from want or need; green signifies hope and also represents the country's forests; and red stands for patriotism and right to freedom.

NORTH MACEDONIA

Adopted on: October 5, 1995
Ratio: 1:2
Capital: Skopje
Independence from Yugoslavia: September 8, 1991
What it means: The design of the 'golden sun' finds mention in the country's national anthem. Red is a traditional colour of Macedonia.

MOLDOVA

Adopted: 1990
Ratio: 1:2
Capital: Chisinau
Independence (from Soviet Union): August 27, 1991
What it means: The flag reflects the tricolour of Romania, of which Moldova was once a part. The emblem is a Roman eagle carrying a yellow cross in its beak, a green olive branch and a yellow sceptre in its talons.

MONTENEGRO

Adopted: July 13, 2004
Ratio: 1:2
Capital: Podgorica
Independence (from Serbia): May 2006
What it means: The flag carries the state coat of arms of a double-headed golden eagle, which was established during the time of Prince Danilo Petrovic Njegos, the founder of the modern State of Montenegrin.

ROMANIA

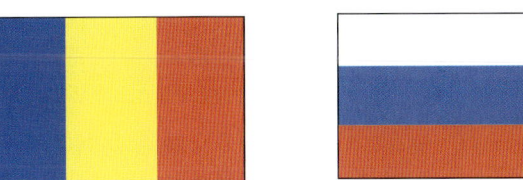

Adopted: 1989
Ratio: 2:3
Capital: Bucharest
Independence from Turkey: May 9, 1877
What it means: The tricolour goes back to Romania's past association with Moldova and Wallachia. The flag came into existence when Moldova and Wallachia united to form Romania, though that flag had horizontal stripes.

RUSSIA

Adopted: 1991
Ratio: 2:3
Capital: Moscow
Independence (from Soviet Union): August 24, 1991
What it means: The white represents nobility, blue, truthfulness and commitment and red, valour and love. The flag was adopted by the Russian Czar, Peter the Great, who was impressed by the Dutch tricolour.

SERBIA

Adopted: August 16, 2004
Ratio: 2:3
Capital: Belgrade
Independence (proclaimed after Montenegro voted for independence): June 5, 2006
What it means: The Pan-Slavic colours red, blue and white stand for unity and independence, as well as freedom and revolutionary ideals.

UKRAINE

Adopted: 1991
Ratio: 2:3
Capital: Kiev (Kyyiv)
Independence (from Soviet Union): August 24, 1991
What it means: The colours were said by Ukranian nationalists to symbolise blue skies over golden wheat fields of the Steppes plains and this has become de facto.

THE MIDDLE EAST

Deserts define much of the Middle East landscape. Iran is largely a central desert plateau, surrounded by soaring mountain ranges. Nearly two-fifths of Iraq too is desert. Kuwait and Qatar, again, are largely desert. Saudi Arabia is largely uninhabited and includes the world's largest sand area, the Rub' al-Khali (the Empty Quarter). Turkey, in contrast, is primarily mountainous and boasts coastlines along the Aegean, the Mediterranean and the Black seas.

Ankara
TURKEY
CYPRUS
Nicosia
SYRIA
LEBANON
Beirut
Damascus
Jerusalem
ISRAEL
Amman
JORDAN
Baghdad
IRAQ
Caspian Sea
Tehran
IRAN
KUWAIT
Kuwait City
Riyadh
Manama
QATAR
BAHRAIN
SAUDI ARABIA
Doha
Abu Dhabi
U.A.E.
Muscat
OMAN
Sana'a
YEMEN

BAHRAIN

Adopted: 1932
Ratio: 3:5
Capital: Manama
Independence from the United Kingdom: August 15, 1971
What it means: Red and white are traditional colours of the Persian Gulf states.

CYPRUS

Adopted: 1960
Ratio: 3:5
Capital: Nicosia
Independence from the United Kingdom: August 16, 1960
What it means: The olive branches symbolise the hope for peace between the island's Greek and Turkish communities. The copper-coloured outline of the island's map is for its name, which is Greek for 'copper'.

IRAN

Adopted: 1980
Ratio: 4:7
Capital: Tehran
Independence: April 1, 1979
What it means: The Arabic phrase Allahu Akbar ('God is great') is repeated 22 times along the edges of the green and red bands. The coat of arms can be taken as a stylised Arabic representation of the word Allah.

IRAQ

Adopted: 2008
Ratio: 1:2
Capital: Baghdad
Independence from League of Nations mandate under British control: October 3, 1932
What it means: The phrase Allahu Akbar is incorporated between the stars. Red, green, white and black are the traditional colours across the Arab world.

ISRAEL

Adopted: 1948
Ratio: 8:11
Capital: Jerusalem
Independence from League of Nations mandate under British control: May 14, 1948
What it means: The six-pointed star is known as the Magen David (Star of David) and is supposed to symbolise King David's shield. Blue and white are taken from the traditional Jewish prayer shawl.

JORDAN

Adopted: 1928
Ratio: 1:2
Capital: Amman
Independence from League of Nations mandate under British control: May 25, 1946
What it means: The hoist-side triangle is symbolic of the Great Arab Revolt of 1916. The seven-pointed star signifies the opening seven verses of the Qur'an.

KUWAIT

Adopted: 1961
Ratio: 1:2
Capital: Kuwait City
Independence from the United Kingdom: June 19, 1961
What it means: Green stands for the fertile land, white for purity, red for the blood of the enemy, and black for the enemy's defeat.

LEBANON

Adopted: 1943
Ratio: 2:3
Capital: Beirut
Independence from League of Nations mandate under French control: November 22, 1943
What it means: The cedar tree has traditionally been a symbol for immortality, strength and wealth.

OMAN

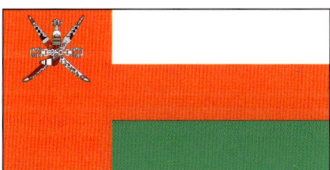

Adopted: 1995
Ratio: Usually 1:2
Capital: Muscat
Independence (the Portuguese were driven out): 1650
What it means: The coat of arms is a dagger in its sheath superimposed on two crossed swords in their holders.

QATAR

Adopted: 1949
Ratio: 11:28
Capital: Doha (Ad-Dawhah)
Independence from the United Kingdom: September 3, 1971
What it means: It is said that the original red dye on the flag got altered into maroon in the Qatar sun! The flag looks similar to that of Bahrain, since Qatar was once a part of Bahrain.

SAUDI ARABIA

Adopted: 1973
Ratio: 2:3
Capital: Riyadh
Independence (unification of the kingdom): September 23, 1932
What it means: Green is a traditional colour in Islamic flags. The Arabic inscription reads: "There is no god but Allah; Muhammad is the prophet of God."

SYRIA

Adopted: 1980
Ratio: 2:3
Capital: Damascus
Independence from League of Nations mandate under French control: April 17, 1946
What it means: The stars represent Syria and Egypt, which were briefly united in 1958 to form the United Arab Republic. The colours are based on the Arab Liberation Flag.

TURKEY

Adopted: 1936
Ratio: Approximately 2:3
Capital: Ankara
Independence (republic declared): October 29, 1923
What it means: The crescent and the star are symbols of Islam.

UNITED ARAB EMIRATES

Adopted: 1971
Ratio: 1:2
Capital: Abu Dhabi
Independence from the United Kingdom: December 2, 1971
What it means: Incorporates the traditional Arab colours of unity and nationalism.

YEMEN

Adopted: 1990
Ratio: 2:3
Capital: Sana'a
Independence (republic declared with the union of North Yemen and South Yemen): May 22, 1990
What it means: The flag was adopted upon the unification of North and South Yemen.

WESTERN AND SOUTHERN
ASIA

Afghanistan, Armenia, Bhutan and Nepal in, Western Asia, are landlocked countries. Rugged mountains make for some of the world's most difficult terrain in the rest of this region.

AFGHANISTAN

Adopted: 2002
Ratio: 1:2
Capital: Kabul
Independence (from U.K. control over foreign affairs): August 19, 1919
What it means: The coat of arms found in the centre of the flag incorporates a mosque encircled by sheaves of wheat and an Islamic inscription.

ARMENIA

Adopted: 1990
Ratio: 1:2
Capital: Yerevan
Independence (from Soviet Union): September 21, 1991
What it means: Red is said to be symbolic of the blood shed by Armenians in their freedom struggle; blue of their skies and hope; and orange of hard work.

AZERBAIJAN

Adopted: 1991
Ratio: 1:2
Capital: Baku
Independence (from Soviet Union): August 30, 1991
What it means: The crescent and the star are symbols of Islam. The eight-pointed stars are thought to represent the eight traditional Turkic peoples.

BANGLADESH

Adopted: 1972
Ratio: 6:10
Capital: Dhaka
Independence (from Pakistan): March 26, 1971
What it means: The disc symbolises the 'rising sun of a new country,' and the colour red symbolises the blood that was shed in the struggle for independence.

AZERBAIJAN

GEORGIA

T'bilisi

Yerevan

Caspian Sea

Baku

ARMENIA

Nur-Sultan

KAZAKHSTAN

Ashgabat

UZBEKISTAN

Tashkent

TURKMENISTAN

Bishkek

KYRGYZSTAN

Dushanbe

TAJIKISTAN

Kabul

AFGHANISTAN

Islamabad

NEPAL

Kathmandu

BHUTAN

Thimphu

PAKISTAN

New Delhi

Dhaka

INDIA

BANGLADESH

MALDIVES

Colombo

Male

SRI LANKA

BHUTAN

Adopted: 1969
Ratio: 2:3
Capital: Thimphu
Independence from India:
August 8, 1949
What it means: The 'thunder' dragon at the centre is the country's national emblem. White is a symbol of purity and loyalty, yellow of the king's power and orange of Buddhist religious practices and monastries.

GEORGIA

Adopted: 2004
Ratio: 2:3
Capital: T'bilisi
Independence from Soviet Union:
April 9, 1991
What it means: The central cross connects all four sides of the flag, with each corner featuring the bolnur-katskhuri crosses. The five-cross theme dates back to the 14th century.

INDIA

Adopted: 1947
Ratio: 2:3
Capital: New Delhi
Independence (from the United Kingdom): August 15, 1947
What it means: The orange (courage and sacrifice), white (peace and truth) and green (faith and chivalry) flag features a 24-spoked Buddhist charka ('Wheel of the Law') at the centre. This wheel stands for non-violence.

KAZAKHSTAN

Adopted: June 4, 1992
Ratio: Approximately 1:2
Capital: Nur-Sultan
Independence from the Soviet Union:
December 16, 1991
What it means: Traditional Kazakh ornamentation is featured on the hoist side. A golden steppe eagle in flight is depicted below the shining sun.

KYRGYZSTAN

Adopted on: March 3, 1992
Ratio: Approximately 3:5
Capital: Bishkek
Independence from the Soviet Union:
August 31, 1991
What it means: The red background is said to have been adopted from the flag carried by the famed Kyrgyz hero, Manas the Noble. The 40 rays of the sun are symbolic of the tribes that the leader helped unite to form the nation.

MALDIVES

Adopted: 1965
Ratio: 2:3
Capital: Male
Independence (from the United Kingdom): July 26, 1965
What it means: Red was the colour of the country's first flag. The green panel with a crescent is symbolic of Islam.

NEPAL

Adopted: 1962
Ratio: 4:3
Capital: Kathmandu
Independence (unified by Prithvi Narayan Shah): 1768
What it means: Two triangles overlap, one with a crescent moon and the other bearing a 12-pointed sun. Red is the colour of the national flower, the rhododendron. The blue stands for peace.

PAKISTAN

Adopted: 1947
Ratio: 2:3
Capital: Islamabad
Independence (from the United Kingdom): August 14, 1947
What it means: The traditional symbols of Islam are used. The white represents the country's non-Muslim population. The star is symbolic of knowledge and light, and the crescent, of progress.

SRI LANKA

Adopted: 1978
Ratio: 1:2
Capital: Sri Jayewardenepura Kotte
Independence (from the United Kingdom): February 4, 1948
What it means: The dark-red rectangle has a lion holding a sword, and four bo leaves, associated with Buddhism, at the corners. The thinner green and orange panels represent the minority Islamic and Tamil communities.

TAJIKISTAN

Adopted on: November 24, 1992
Ratio: 1:2
Capital: Dushanbe
Independence from Soviet Union:
September 9, 1991
What it means: The centred crown and the arc of seven gold stars are said to symbolise unity among the country's various social classes.

TURKMENISTAN

Adopted on: February 19, 1997
Ratio: 1:2
Capital: Ashgabat
Independence from the Soviet Union:
October 27, 1991
What it means: The five carpet motifs on the hoist-side are representative of the country's rich, traditional carpet industry.

UZBEKISTAN

Adopted on: November 18, 1991
Ratio: Approximately 1:2
Capital: Tashkent
Independence from the Soviet Union:
September 1, 1991
What it means: The 12 stars are for the 12 months in the year as well as for the constellations in the zodiac.

EAST AND SOUTHEAST
ASIA

NORTH KOREA
JAPAN
Tokyo
Ulaanbaatar
MONGOLIA
P'yongyang
Seoul
SOUTH KOREA
Beijing
PEOPLE'S REPUBLIC OF CHINA
Chinese Taipei
Hanoi
LAOS
MYANMAR (BURMA)
Vientiane
Manila
PHILIPPINES
Naypyidaw
VIETNAM
Bangkok
CAMBODIA
Phnom Penh
THAILAND
Bandar Seri Begawan
BRUNEI
MALAYSIA
Kuala Lumpur
Singapore
SINGAPORE
INDONESIA
Jakarta
Dili
EAST TIMOR

East and Southeast Asia are located between the Pacific and Indian oceans. China, the largest of the Asian countries, occupies a major chunk of the East Asian landmass. Indonesia comprises over 13,600 islands, while the Philippines has about 7,100 islands and islets spreading out in a triangle.

BRUNEI

Adopted: 1959
Ratio: 1:2
Capital: Bandar Seri Begawan
Independence (from the United Kingdom): January 1, 1984
What it means: The yellow represents the Sultan of Brunei, while the white and black stand for the two chief ministers. The coat of arms features a crescent, below which a ribbon has the inscription 'Brunei, abode of peace'.

CAMBODIA

Adopted: 1993
Ratio: 2:3
Capital: Phnom Penh
Independence from France: November 9, 1953
What it means: Red and blue are the country's traditional colours. At the centre is the three-towered temple complex of Angkor Wat, making it the only national flag to feature a building.

PEOPLE'S REPUBLIC OF CHINA

Adopted: 1949
Ratio: 2:3
Capital: Beijing
Independence (People's Republic established): October 1, 1949
What it means: Red, besides being the Chinese traditional colour, represents the communist revolution. The large star stands for the Chinese Communist Party, with the other four smaller ones denoting the four social classes.

EAST TIMOR

Adopted: 2002
Ratio: 1:2
Capital: Dili
Independence (recognised; from Portugal): May 20, 2002
What it means: The colour yellow represents centuries of colonial repression, black stands for uncertainities that need to be overcome and red is for freedom struggle. The white star is the 'light that guides'.

INDONESIA

Adopted: 1945
Ratio: 2:3
Capital: Jakarta
Independence (declared; from the Netherlands): August 17, 1945
What it means: The flag goes back to the 13th century, when the Majapahit Empire used a similar flag. Indonesians consider the traditional colours of red (courage) and white (honesty) holy.

JAPAN

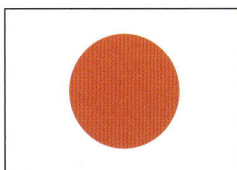

Adopted: 1870
Ratio: 2:3
Capital: Tokyo
Independence (traditional founding): 660 BC
What it means: The red disc of the sun (Hinomaru) is a traditional Japanese symbol. The white stands for honesty and purity.

KOREA, NORTH

Adopted: 1948
Ratio: 1:2
Capital: P'yongyang
Independence (from Japan): August 15, 1945
What it means: The red stripe and the star represent the communist ideology. The blue and white stripes, respectively, symbolise peace and purity.

KOREA, SOUTH

Adopted: 1950
Ratio: 2:3
Capital: Seoul
Independence (from Japan): August 15, 1945
What it means: The flag is called Taegukki. The yin-yang symbol stands for unity. The four sets of black bars represent sun, moon, earth and heaven.

LAOS

Adopted: 1975
Ratio: 2:3
Capital: Vientiane
Independence (from France): July 19, 1949
What it means: The white disc on a blue field is believed to be symbolic of the moon glowing over the Mekong River.

MALAYSIA

Adopted: 1963
Ratio: 1:2
Capital: Kuala Lumpur
Independence (from the United Kingdom): August 31, 1957
What it means: The 14 stripes and 14 points of the star represent the original 14 states of Malaysia. Since Singapore left the federation in 1965, the 14th stripe and point is said to represent the Malaysian government.

MONGOLIA

Adopted: 1940
Ratio: 1:2
Capital: Ulaanbaatar
Independence (from China): July 11, 1921
What it means: The sky blue is Mongolia's national colour. The traditional emblem of soyonbo is featured in the red bar on the hoist side.

MYANMAR (BURMA)

Adopted: 1974
Ratio: 1:2
Capital: Naypyidaw (as of 2005)
Independence (from the United Kingdom): January 4, 1948
What it means: The new flag design of Myanmar goes back to the 1943 yellow-green-red tricolour but replacing the peacock with a white star set in the centre of the flag.

PHILIPPINES, THE

Adopted: 1898
Ratio: Usually 1:2
Capital: Manila
Independence (from Spain): June 12, 1898
What it means: The three stars are for Luzon, Mindanao and Visayan. The sun symbolises independence, and its eight rays, the provinces that rose against the Spanish rule. Blue and red stand for patriotism and courage.

SINGAPORE

Adopted: 1959
Ratio: 2:3
Capital: Singapore
Independence (from Malaysian Federation): August 9, 1965
What it means: The white crescent is symbolic of the young nation. The five stars stand for democracy, peace, progress, justice and equality. Red signifies universal brotherhood and white, purity and virtue.

THAILAND

Adopted: 1917
Ratio: 2:3
Capital: Bangkok
Independence (traditional founding): 1238
What it means: The common symbolisms are – red for the blood sacrificed by the people for their country, white for the purity of Buddhism, and blue for the monarchy.

VIETNAM

Adopted: 1955
Ratio: 2:3
Capital: Hanoi
Independence (from France): September 2, 1945
What it means: The main classes of workers are represented by the five points of the star.

WEST AFRICA

West Africa is the westernmost region of the African continent. The northwestern region – comprised of Morocco (including Western Sahara), Algeria, Tunisia (and sometimes Lybia) – is known as the Maghreb, from an Arabic word meaning "western". West Africa incorporates a great span of cultures, geography and bioregions. A large area of west Africa is dominated by the Sahara desert, which spreads through nearly all of northern Africa.

ALGERIA

Adopted: 1962
Ratio: 2:3
Capital: Algiers
Independence (from France): July 5, 1962
What it means: The colour green, and the crescent and star are Islamic symbols.

BENIN

Adopted: 1959
Ratio: 2:3
Capital: Porto-Novo
Independence (from France): August 1, 1960
What it means: Features pan-African colours, symbolic of African unity.

BURKINA FASO

Adopted: 1984
Ratio: Approximately 2:3
Capital: Ouagadougou
Independence (from France): August 5, 1960
What it means: The red is symbolic of the 1984 revolution.

CAMEROON

Adopted: 1975
Ratio: Approximately 2:3
Capital: Yaoundé
Independence (from UN trusteeship): January 1, 1960
What it means: The central star symbolises national unity.

CAPE VERDE

Adopted: 1992
Ratio: 3:5
Capital: Praia
Independence (from Portugal): July 5, 1975
What it means: The blue field and the stars represent the 10 main islands.

CÔTE D'IVOIRE (IVORY COAST)

Adopted: 1959
Ratio: Approximately 2:3
Capital: Yamoussoukro
Independence (from France): August 7, 1960
What it means: The flag symbolises dynamic growth, peace and hope.

EQUATORIAL GUINEA

Adopted: 1979
Ratio: Approximately 2:3
Capital: Malabo
Independence (from Spain): October 12, 1968
What it means: The six stars represent the five principal islands and the mainland.

GABON

Adopted: 1960
Ratio: 3:4
Capital: Libreville
Independence (from France): August 17, 1960
What it means: The green and yellow signify the country's natural wealth, while the blue represents the coast.

GAMBIA

Adopted: 1965
Ratio: 2:3
Capital: Banjul
Independence (from the United Kingdom): February 18, 1965
What it means: Red, blue and green represent Gambia's natural reserves.

GHANA

Adopted: 1957
Ratio: 2:3
Capital: Accra
Independence (from the United Kingdom): March 6, 1957
What it means: The black star stands for 'African freedom'.

GUINEA
Adopted: 1958
Ratio: 2:3
Capital: Conakry
Independence (from France): October 2, 1958
What it means: The flag incorporates pan-African colours.

GUINEA-BISSAU

Adopted: 1973
Ratio: Approximately 1:2
Capital: Bissau
Independence (declared; from Portugal): September 24, 1973
What it means: The black star stands for the people's right to freedom.

LIBERIA

Adopted: 1847
Ratio: 10:19
Capital: Monrovia
Independence: July 26, 1847
What it means: The stripes are for the men who signed the Liberian Declaration of Independence.

WESTERN SAHARA (DISPUTED)

MOROCCO — Rabat
Algiers — Tunis
TUNISIA
ALGERIA
BURKINA FASO
MAURITANIA
Nouakchott
CAPE VERDE
Praia
SENEGAL
Dakar
GAMBIA
Banjul
Bissau
GUINEA-BISSAU
GUINEA
Conakry
Freetown
SIERRA LEONE
Monrovia
LIBERIA
IVORY COAST
Yamoussoukro
Bamako
MALI
Ouagadougou
GHANA
TOGO
BENIN
Accra
Lomé
Porto-Novo
NIGER
Niamey
NIGERIA
Abuja
CAMEROON
Yaoundé
Malabo
EQUATORIAL GUINEA
São Tomé
SÃO TOMÉ AND PRÍNCIPE
Libreville
GABON

MALI

Adopted: 1961
Ratio: 2:3
Capital: Bamako
Independence (from France): September 22, 1960
What it means: The Mali flag uses pan-African colours.

MAURITANIA

Adopted: 2017
Ratio: 2:3
Capital: Nouakchott
Independence (from France): November 28, 1960
What it means: The green field, the star and the crescent represent Islam.

MOROCCO

Adopted: 1915
Ratio: 2:3
Capital: Rabat
Independence (from France): March 2, 1956
What it means: Red is for the descendants of Prophet Muhammad.

NIGER

Adopted: 1959
Ratio: Approximately 6:7
Capital: Niamey
Independence (from France): August 3, 1960
What it means: The orange disc symbolises the sun.

NIGERIA

Adopted: 1960
Ratio: 1:2
Capital: Abuja
Independence (from the United Kingdom): October 1, 1960
What it means: White reminds of peace and unity, and green of the fertile land.

SÃO TOMÉ AND PRÍNCIPE

Adopted: 1975
Ratio: 1:2
Capital: São Tomé
Independence (from Portugal): July 12, 1975
What it means: The red triangle is a symbol for the freedom struggle.

SENEGAL

Adopted: 1960
Ratio: Approximately 2:3
Capital: Dakar
Independence (from France): April 4, 1960
What it means: The green star is symbolic of hope and unity.

SIERRA LEONE

Adopted: 1961
Ratio: 2:3
Capital: Freetown
Independence (from the United Kingdom): April 27, 1961
What it means: Green stands for agricultural, white for unity and justice, and blue for the natural harbour at Freetown.

TOGO

Adopted: 1960
Ratio: Approximately 3:5
Capital: Lomé
Independence (from French-administered UN trusteeship): April 27, 1960
What it means: The red field represents the values of love, loyalty and charity. It features the 'Star of Hope' and emphasises purity and national unity.

TUNISIA

Adopted: 1835
Ratio: 2:3
Capital: Tunis
Independence (from France): March 20, 1956
What it means: The crescent and star are traditional symbols of Islam.

EAST AFRICA

The Great Rift Valley is a vast geological feature stretching from Ethiopia to Mozambique in East Africa. About 160 kilometres (100 miles) east of the East African Rift System (of which the Great Rift Valley is a branch) is Kilimanjaro, which, at 5,895 metres (19,340 feet), is the highest point in Africa.

BURUNDI

Adopted: 1967
Ratio: 3:5
Capital: Gitega
Independence (from UN trusteeship under Belgian administration): July 1, 1962
What it means: The three stars represent the three main ethnic groups of the country – the Hutu, Tutsi and Twa.

CENTRAL AFRICAN REPUBLIC

Adopted: 1958
Ratio: Approximately 3:5
Capital: Bangui
Independence (from the United Kingdom): August 13, 1960
What it means: The red stripe symbolises the bond between Africans and Europeans. The yellow star expresses hope for a bright future.

CHAD

Adopted: 1959
Ratio: 2:3
Capital: N'Djamena
Independence (from France): August 11, 1960
What it means: Uses the pan-African colours of red and yellow with the French tricolour's blue and red.

DEMOCRATIC REPUBLIC OF THE CONGO (ZAIRE)

Adopted: 2006
Ratio: 2:3
Capital: Kinshasa
Independence (from France): June 30, 1960
What it means: The six stars along the hoist were incorporated to represent the original provinces of Congo.

DJIBOUTI

Adopted: 1977
Ratio: 2:3
Capital: Djibouti
Independence (from France): June 27, 1977
What it means: Blue represents the Issa people, and green the Afar people. The white triangle bears a red star for national unity.

Map labels:
Tripoli, LIBYA, Cairo, EGYPT, SUDAN, Khartoum, ERITREA, Asmara, DJIBOUTI, Djibouti, CHAD, N'Djamena, SOMALIA, Addis Ababa, ETHIOPIA, CENTRAL AFRICAN REPUBLIC, SOUTH SUDAN, Bangui, Juba, Mogadishu, REPUBLIC OF THE CONGO, UGANDA, KENYA, Kampala, Nairobi, Victoria, DEMOCRATIC REPUBLIC OF THE CONGO, SEYCHELLES, Brazzaville, Kinshasa, RWANDA, Kigali, BURUNDI, Gitega

EGYPT

Adopted: 1984
Ratio: 2:3
Capital: Cairo
Independence (from the United Kingdom): February 28, 1922
What it means: Pan-African colours are used. The coat of arms is the golden eagle of the 12th-century ruler Saladin, who fought in the Crusades.

ERITREA

Adopted: 1995
Ratio: 1:2
Capital: Asmara
Independence (from Ethiopia): May 24, 1991
What it means: The green, blue and red are the party colours of the Eritrean People's Liberation Front (EPLF), who had led the independence struggle. The olive branch circled by a wreath was inspired by the flag of the United Nations and signify the country's autonomy.

ETHIOPIA

Adopted: 1996
Ratio: 1:2
Capital: Addis Ababa
Independence: March 1, 1896
What it means: The green, gold and red of the flag of Ethiopia (the oldest independent state in Africa) were so often adopted by emerging independent African states that they became known as the Pan-African colours. The star stands for unity among the Ethiopian nationalities.

KENYA

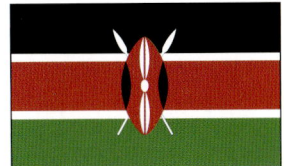

Adopted: 1963
Ratio: 2:3
Capital: Nairobi
Independence (from the United Kingdom): December 12, 1963
What it means: Black, red and green belonged to the Kenya African Union (KAU) party. White was added to represent the democractic party and national unity. The Masai shield and two crossed spears stand for national pride and tradition.

LIBYA

Adopted: 1977
Ratio: 1:2
Capital: Tripoli
Independence (from Italy): December 24, 1951
What it means: The only national flag to use a single colour.

REPUBLIC OF THE CONGO

Adopted: 1958
Ratio: 2:3
Capital: Brazzaville
Independence (from France): August 15, 1960
What it means: Uses the pan-African colours which symbolise African independence and unity.

RWANDA

Adopted: 2001
Ratio: Approximately 2:3
Capital: Kigali
Independence (from Belgium-administered UN trusteeship): July 1, 1962
What it means: Blue bears the message of happiness and peace. Yellow stands for economic progress, while green is symbolic of prosperity.

SEYCHELLES

Adopted: 1996
Ratio: 1:2
Capital: Victoria
Independence (from the United Kingdom): June 29, 1976
What it means: The red, white and green are the colors of the Seychelles People's United Party (SPUP). The blue and yellow are of the Democratic Party.

SOMALIA

Adopted: 1954
Ratio: 2:3
Capital: Mogadishu
Independence (from the United Kingdom and Italy): July 1, 1960
What it means: The blue field is inspired by the United Nations (UN) flag. The 'Star of Unity' is symbolic of the Somali people scattered across places such as Djibouti, Ethiopia and Kenya.

SOUTH SUDAN

Adopted: 2011
Ratio: 1:2
Capital: Juba
Independence (from Sudan): 2011
What it means: This flag has six colours. The black stands for the black African ancestry of the South Sudanese. The white colour is a symbol of peace and goodwill. Red stands for the blood and sacrifice. Green stands for agriculture, natural wealth and prosperity. The blue triangle is symbolic of the Nile River which flows through the land. Yellow is a symbol of hope.

SUDAN

Adopted: 1970
Ratio: 1:2
Capital: Khartoum
Independence (from Egypt and the United Kingdom): January 1, 1956
What it means: Red stands for socialism and progress, and white for peace and hope. Black recalls the name of the country (sudan is Arabic for 'black').

UGANDA

Adopted: 1962
Ratio: 2:3
Capital: Kampala
Independence (from the United Kingdom): October 9, 1962
What it means: The striped colours are from the tricolour of the Uganda People's Congress (UPC). The crested crane is the national symbol.

CENTRAL AND SOUTHERN
AFRICA

Central Africa lies across the Equator. The terrain consists of wide plateaus, which may reach a height of about 914 metres (3,000 feet) near the Angolan border. Central Africa's highest point is Margherita Peak – at 5,119 metres (16,795 feet). It is located on the eastern fringe of the Rift Valley.

Southern Africa too features a high interior plateau that consists of rolling grasslands. However, the monotony of the plateau is broken by the Kalahari desert and the Great Escarpment, a series of mountain ranges that run parallel to a narrow coastal strip. The Zambezi and the Limpopo are the largest rivers in the region.

ANGOLA

Adopted: 1975
Ratio: 2:3
Capital: Luanda
Independence (from Portugal): November 11, 1975
What it means: The machete and the cogwheel in the central yellow emblem stand for agriculture and industry, while the star is symbolic of progress. The red colour represents the blood shed during the freedom struggle and the black stands for Africa.

BOTSWANA

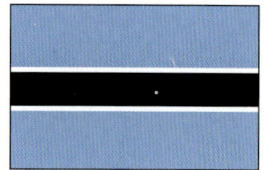

Adopted: 1966
Ratio: 2:3
Capital: Gaborone
Independence (from the United Kingdom): September 30, 1966
What it means: The blue background is symbolic of water and life, and the black-and-white centre, inspired by the coat of the national animal, zebra, signifies racial equality among the people.

COMOROS

Adopted: 2001 (current flag)
Ratio: 2:3
Capital: Moroni
Independence (from France): July 6, 1975
What it means: The crescent and stars are Islamic symbols. The four stars represent the main islands of the union.

LESOTHO

Adopted: 2006
Ratio: 9:14
Capital: Maseru
Independence (from the United Kingdom): October 4, 1966
What it means: The white triangle symbolises peace and features an outline of a shield with a spear and a traditional club. The green triangle stands for prosperity, while the blue band represents rain.

MADAGASCAR

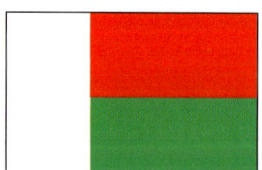

Adopted: 1958
Ratio: 2:3
Capital: Antananarivo
Independence (from France): June 26, 1960
What it means: Red and white are the traditional colours of Madagascar. Green is believed to recall the country's former peasant class (Hova).

MALAWI

Adopted: 1964
Ratio: 2:3
Capital: Lilongwe
Independence (from France): July 6, 1964
What it means: Black (African heritage), red (blood of martyrs) and green (the land) are the colours of the Malawi Congress Party. The rising sun represents dawn of hope and freedom for the whole of Africa.

MAURITIUS

Adopted: 1968
Ratio: 2:3
Capital: Port Louis
Independence (from the United Kingdom): March 12, 1968
What it means: Red stands for the independence movement, blue for the Indian Ocean, yellow for the 'light of freedom shining over the island,' and green for the rich vegetation.

MOZAMBIQUE

Adopted: 1983
Ratio: Approximately 2:3
Capital: Maputo
Independence (from Portugal): June 25, 1975
What it means: The yellow star bears an open book (education) overlaid by a hoe (peasantry) and rifle (defence of the land).

SOUTH AFRICA

Adopted: 1994
Ratio: 2:3
Capital: Pretoria, Cape Town and Bloemfontein
Independence (from the United Kingdom): May 31, 1910; proclaimed a republic on May 31, 1961
What it means: The Y-shape symbolises 'converging of paths' and unification. The red, white and blue were taken from the colours of the 19th-century Boer Republics. The yellow, black and green are from the African National Congress (ANC) flag.

TANZANIA
Dar es Salaam
Luanda
ANGOLA
MALAWI
Lilongwe
ZAMBIA
Lusaka
Harare
ZIMBABWE
MOZAMBIQUE
Moroni
COMOROS
MADAGASCAR
Antananarivo
Port Louis
MAURITIUS

NAMIBIA

NAMIBIA
Windhoek
BOTSWANA
Gaborone
Pretoria
Maputo
Mbabane
ESWATINI
Maseru
LESOTHO
SOUTH AFRICA

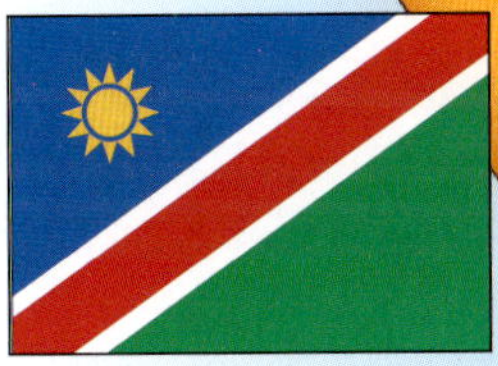

Adopted: 1990
Ratio: 2:3
Capital: Windhoek
Independence (from South African mandate): March 21, 1990
What it means: Blue, red and green were the flag colours of the South West Africa People's Organization (SWAPO), the group that liberated the country in 1990. The sun symbolises life and energy.

ESWATINI

Adopted: 1967
Ratio: 2:3
Capital: Mbabane and Lobamba
Independence (from the United Kingdom): September 6, 1968
What it means: The background is based on the flag that King Sobhuza II gave to the Swazi Pioneer Corps in 1941. The centered Swazi shield features two spears and a staff with hanging feather tassels of the widowbird.

TANZANIA

Adopted: 1964
Ratio: 2:3
Capital: Dar es Salaam
Independence (republic formed by union of Tanganyika and Zanzibar): April 26, 1964
What it means: The green and black were taken from the Tanganyika flag and represent the land and people of Tanzania. The blue, for the sea, came from the Zanzibar flag.

ZAMBIA

Adopted: 1964
Ratio: 2:3
Capital: Lusaka
Independence (from the United Kingdom): October 24, 1964
What it means: The colours belonged to the United Nationalist Independent Party, the main political party during the time Zambia became independent. The eagle, taken from the national coat of arms, is symbolic of freedom and patriotism.

ZIMBABWE

Adopted: 1980
Ratio: 1:2
Capital: Harare
Independence (from the United Kingdom): April 18, 1980
What it means: The Zimbabwe Bird is a national emblem. The triangle stands for peace and the red star denotes the government's socialist ideals.

OCEANIA

Oceania is the name for a group of islands distributed across the Pacific Ocean. It includes over 10,000 islands and is normally divided into the regions of Australasia (Australia and New Zealand), Melanesia, Micronesia and Polynesia. Australia is the world's smallest continent as well as the sixth largest country. An isolated island, New Zealand is separated from its nearest neighbour, Australia, by more than 1,600 km (1,000 miles).

AUSTRALIA

Adopted: 1909
Ratio: 1:2
Capital: Canberra
Independence (federation of U.K. colonies): January 1, 1901
What it means: The Union Jack is featured on the upper hoist side, with the seven-pointed Commonwealth Star below. The five stars on the right half represent the Southern Cross constellation.

FIJI ISLANDS

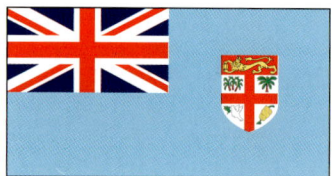

Adopted: 1970
Ratio: 1:2
Capital: Suva
Independence (from the United Kingdom): October 10, 1970
What it means: The blue field is symbolic of the Pacific Ocean. The coat of arms displays a golden British lion, with the panels displaying sugar cane, a palm tree, bananas and the dove of peace.

KIRIBATI

Adopted: 1979
Ratio: 1:2
Capital: Tarawa
Independence (from the United Kingdom): July 12, 1979
What it means: The upper half shows a local frigate bird flying over the rising sun, as a symbol of strength and power at sea. The blue and white bands represent the Pacific Ocean.

MARSHALL ISLANDS

Adopted: 1979
Ratio: 10:19
Capital: Dalap-Uliga-Darrit (on Majuro Atoll)
Independence (from U.S.-administered UN trusteeship): October 21, 1986
What it means: The orange and white signify the country's parallel island chains. The 24-pointed star stands for as many districts of the islands.

MICRONESIA

Adopted: 1978
Ratio: 10:19
Capital: Palikir
Independence (from U.S.-administered UN trusteeship): November 3, 1986
What it means: The four stars stand for the four island groups in the country, centred on a blue field for the Pacific Ocean.

NAURU

Adopted: 1968
Ratio: 1:2
Capital: No official capital
Independence (from Australia-, New Zealand-, and U.K.-administered UN trusteeship): January 31, 1968
What it means: The yellow line represents the Equator, and the 12-pointed star stands for the 12 original tribes of Nauru.

NEW ZEALAND

Adopted: 1902
Ratio: 1:2
Capital: Wellington
Independence (from the United Kingdom): September 26, 1907
What it means: The stars represent the Southern Cross constellation.

PALAU

Adopted: 1981
Ratio: 5:8
Capital: Melekeok
Independence (from U.S.-administered UN trusteeship): October 1, 1994
What it means: Palauans regard the full moon, represented by the disc, auspicious for agriculture.

PAPUA NEW GUINEA

Adopted: 1971
Ratio: 3:4
Capital: Port Moresby
Independence (from Australia-administered UN trusteeship): September 16, 1975
What it means: The five stars stand for the Southern Cross, while the bird-of-paradise is a local symbol. Red and black are native colours.

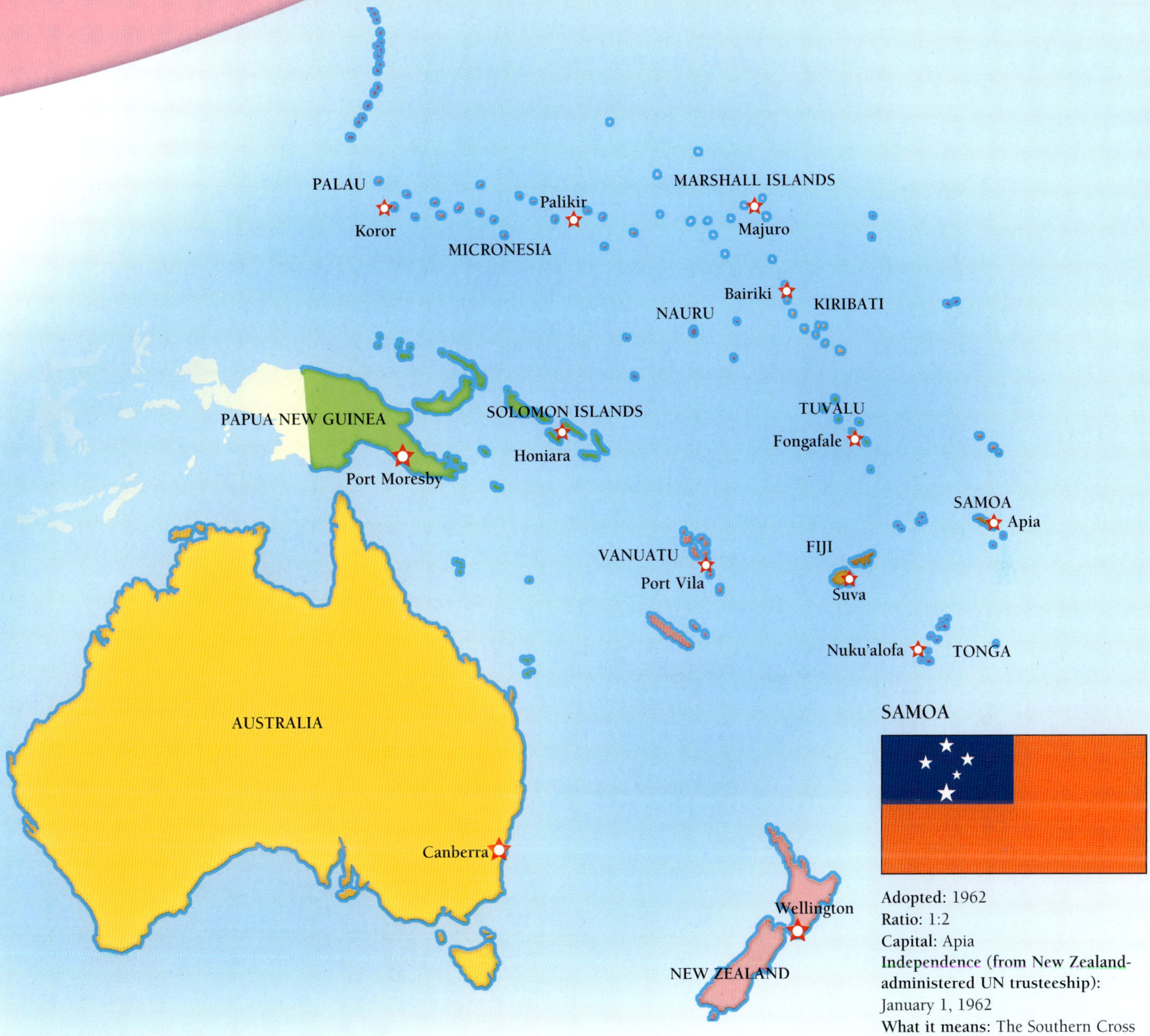

PALAU

Koror

Palikir

MICRONESIA

MARSHALL ISLANDS

Majuro

Bairiki

NAURU

KIRIBATI

PAPUA NEW GUINEA

Port Moresby

SOLOMON ISLANDS

Honiara

TUVALU

Fongafale

SAMOA

Apia

VANUATU

Port Vila

FIJI

Suva

Nuku'alofa

TONGA

AUSTRALIA

Canberra

Wellington

NEW ZEALAND

SAMOA

Adopted: 1962
Ratio: 1:2
Capital: Apia
Independence (from New Zealand-administered UN trusteeship): January 1, 1962
What it means: The Southern Cross emblem is used. Blue stands for freedom and red for courage.

SOLOMON ISLANDS

Adopted: 1977
Ratio: 1:2
Capital: Honiara
Independence (from the United Kingdom): July 7, 1978
What it means: The five white stars represent the country's original provinces. The blue triangle signifies water and the green, the land. The yellow stripe symbolises sunshine.

TONGA

Adopted: 1875
Ratio: 1:2
Capital: Nuku'alofa
Independence (from U.K. protectorate status): June 4, 1970
What it means: The red field is symbolic of the blood shed by Jesus on the cross. The cross stands as a symbol of Christianity, with the white representing purity.

TUVALU

Adopted: 1978
Ratio: 1:2
Capital: Fongafale (on Funafuti Atoll)
Independence (from the United Kingdom): October 1, 1978
What it means: The nine stars represent the nine islands that constitute the country.

VANUATU

Adopted: 1990
Ratio: 3:5
Capital: Port Vila
Independence (from France and the United Kingdom): July 30, 1980
What it means: The Y-shape represents the shape formed by the islands.

UNITED STATES OF
AMERICA

The United States is a federal republic made up of 50 states – 48 of these are connected in one continuous landmass. Alaska and Hawaii do not share their boundaries with any of the other states. Its total area of 9,529,063 sq km (3,679,192 square miles) makes the United States the world's fourth largest country (after Russia, Canada and China).

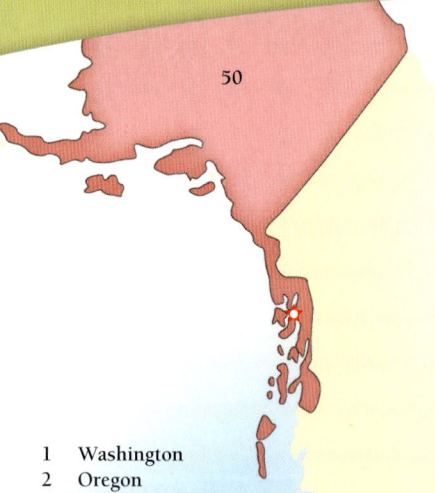

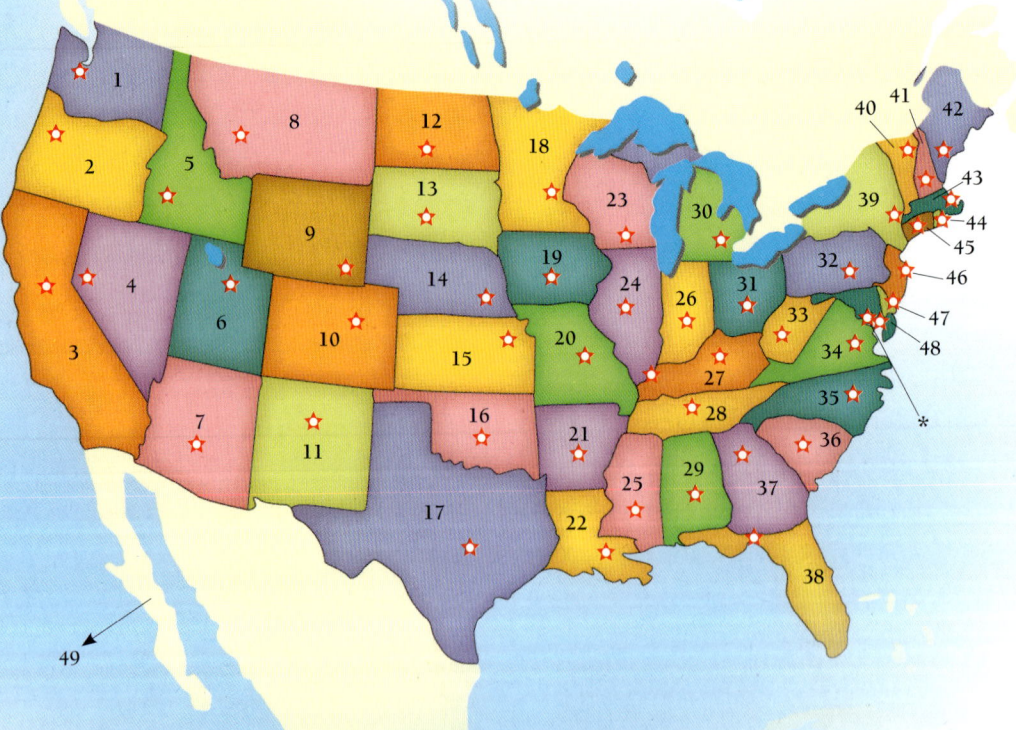

1 Washington
2 Oregon
3 California
4 Nevada
5 Idaho
6 Utah
7 Arizona
8 Montana
9 Wyoming
10 Colorado
11 New Mexico
12 North Dakota
13 South Dakota
14 Nebraska
15 Kansas
16 Oklahoma
17 Texas
18 Minnesota
19 Iowa
20 Missouri
21 Arkansas
22 Louisiana
23 Wisconsin
24 Illinois
25 Mississippi
26 Indiana
27 Kentucky
28 Tennessee
29 Alabama
30 Michigan

31 Ohio
32 Pennsylvania
33 West Virginia
34 Virginia
35 North Carolina
36 South Carolina
37 Georgia
38 Florida
39 New York
40 Vermont
41 New Hampshire
42 Maine
43 Massachusetts
44 Rhode Island
45 Connecticut
46 New Jersey
47 Delaware
48 Maryland
49 Hawaii
50 Alaska
* District of Colombia

Alabama

Adopted: 1895
Ratio: can be square or rectangular
Capital: Montgomery
What it means: Based on the battle flag of the Confederate States during the Civil War.

Alaska

Adopted: 1959
Ratio: 2:3
Capital: Juneau
What it means: A 13-year-old boy, Benny Benson, designed this flag in 1926, depicting the North Star and the Ursa Major constellation.

Arizona

Adopted: 1913
Ratio: 2:3
Capital: Phoenix
What it means: The copper-coloured star represents the copper resources of Arizona.

Arkansas

Adopted: 1913
Ratio: 2:3
Capital: Little Rock
What it means: The diamond shape of the central white emblem symbolises the state's diamond production.

California

Adopted: 1911
Ratio: 2:3
Capital: Sacramento
What it means: The flag bearing a grizzly bear goes back to an 1846 local revolt.

Colorado

Adopted: 1911
Ratio: 2:3
Capital: Denver
What it means: The red 'C' recalls the Spanish word colorado ('red coloured'), from which the name of the state originated.

Connecticut

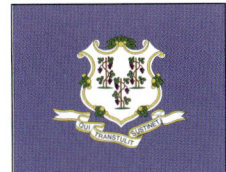

Adopted: 1897
Ratio: 4:5
Capital: Hartford
What it means: The Latin inscription reads "He who transplanted still sustains us." This is based on a psalm.

Delaware

Adopted: 1913
Ratio: 3:4
Capital: Dover
What it means: The date beneath the coat of arms is when Delaware became the first state to formally approve the U.S. Constitution.

Florida

Adopted: 1900
Ratio: 2:3
Capital: Tallahassee
What it means: The flag recalls the Confederate flag of the Civil War. The state seal is at the centre.

Georgia

Adopted: 2003
Ratio: 2:3
Capital: Atlanta
What it means: The 13 stars around the state's coat of arms refer to Georgia as one of the 13 original colonies.

Hawaii

Adopted: 1845
Ratio: 1:2
Capital: Honolulu
What it means: The Union Jack can be traced to the year 1793, when a British army officer made a gift of the flag to the Hawaiian king.

Idaho

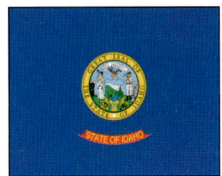

Adopted: 1927
Ratio: 2:3
Capital: Boise
What it means: The flag is based on an earlier military banner.

Illinois

Adopted: 1915
Ratio: 3:5
Capital: Sacramento
What it means: The dates 1818 and 1868, respectively, stand for statehood and the first time the state seal was used.

Indiana

Adopted: 1917
Ratio: 2:3
Capital: Indianapolis
What it means: The 19 stars around the gold torch recall Indiana's status as the 19th state to join the Union.

Iowa

Adopted: 1921
Ratio: 2:3
Capital: Des Moines
What it means: The flag recalls the French tricolour – Iowa was once a part of French Louisiana.

Kansas

Adopted: 1925
Ratio: 3:5
Capital: Topeka
What it means: The sunflower was adopted as the state's floral emblem in 1903.

Kentucky

Adopted: 1918
Ratio: 2:3
Capital: Frankfort
What it means: The theme of national unity is reflected in the state seal.

Louisiana

Adopted: 2010
Ratio: 2:3
Capital: Baton Rouge
What it means: The pelican represents the spirit of self-sacrifice.

Maine

Adopted: 1909
Ratio: 2:3
Capital: Augusta
What it means: The coat of arms depicts a farmer and a sailor representing the agricultural and shipbuilding industries. The Latin motto means, "I direct."

Maryland

Adopted: 1904
Ratio: 2:3
Capital: Annapolis
What it means: The flag retains British heraldic symbols.

Massachusetts

Adopted: 1908
Ratio: 2:3
Capital: Boston
What it means: The Latin motto reads "By the sword we seek peace, but peace only under liberty." The coat of arms on a white background served many Massachusetts regiments.

Michigan

Adopted: 1911
Ratio: 2:3
Capital: Lansing
What it means: The state seal features the bald eagle, a shield, an elk and a moose. There are three Latin mottoes: "One out of many," "I will defend," and "If you seek a pleasant peninsula, look about you."

Minnesota

Adopted: 1893
Ratio: 7:11
Capital: St Paul
What it means: The state's motto, 'Star of the north', is shown on the red ribbon. Minnesota was the northernmost state in the Union before Alaska joined it.

Mississippi

Adopted: 2021
Ratio: 2:3
Capital: Jackson
What it means: The flag has a white magnolia blossom and the words "In God We Trust". The magnolia is the symbol of the state's hospitality, hope and rebirth.

Missouri

Adopted: 1913
Ratio: 10:17
Capital: Jefferson City
What it means: The Latin motto reads: "The welfare of the people shall be the supreme law."

Montana

Adopted: 1905
Ratio: 2:3
Capital: Helena
What it means: The state seal depicts the state's scenic landscape – the Rocky Mountains, the Great Falls, a river and forests. The plough, and the crossed pick and shovel are symbolic of agriculture and mining.

Nebraska

Adopted: 1963
Ratio: 3:5
Capital: Lincoln
What it means: The 1867 state seal is themed around Nebraska's agricultural and industrial development.

Nevada

Adopted: 1929
Ratio: 2:3
Capital: Carson City
What it means: The sagebrush is Nevada's state flower. The phrase 'Battle born' recalls Nevada's admission to the Union during the Civil War (1861-65).

New Hampshire

Adopted: 1909
Ratio: 2:3
Capital: Concord
What it means: The state seal was adopted in 1784 and it features the frigate Raleigh, which was built in 1776 and was one of the first ships in the nation's navy.

New Jersey

Adopted: 1896
Ratio: 2:3
Capital: Trenton
What it means: The field of buff (light tan) was taken from the uniform colour worn by New Jersey troops in the Revolutionary War (1775-83).

New Mexico

Adopted: 1925
Ratio: 2:3
Capital: Santa Fe
What it means: The sun symbol belonged to the Zia Pueblo Indians. Yellow and red were inspired by the flag of Spain, which controlled New Mexico until the beginning of the 19th century.

New York

Adopted: 1901
Ratio: 1:2
Capital: Albany
What it means: The coat of arms features a sun symbol and the two supporters of the shield – Liberty (on the left) and Justice.

North Carolina

Adopted: 1885
Ratio: 2:3
Capital: Raleigh
What it means: May 20, 1775, recalls the first meeting of North Carolina citizens proclaiming their freedom from Great Britain.

North Dakota

Adopted: 1911
Ratio: 2:3
Capital: Bismarck
What it means: The flag was earlier used by the state's military regiments.

Ohio

Adopted: 1902
Ratio: 5:8
Capital: Columbus
What it means: The swallow-tailed shape of the flag was probably inspired by a standard carried by the U.S. cavalry during the Civil War.

Oklahoma

Adopted: 1907
Ratio: 2:3
Capital: Oklahoma City
What it means: The bison-hide shield belongs to the Osage Indians. An olive branch and a Native American peace pipe are emblems of peace. The four small crosses are common motifs in Native American art and stand for high ideals.

Oregon

Adopted: 1925
Ratio: 3:5
Capital: Salem
What it means: The date commemorates Oregon's admission into the Union. Elements from the state seal are used. The reverse side depicts the beaver in golden yellow.

Pennsylvania

Adopted: 1907
Ratio: 2:3
Capital: Harrisburg
What it means: The coat of arms (from 1777) features the official seal of the William Penn family, the founders of Pennsylvania.

Rhode Island

Adopted: 1897
Ratio: 1:1
Capital: Providence
What it means: The centred anchor (symbolic of hope) has been the emblem of Rhode Island for centuries.

South Carolina

Adopted: 1861
Ratio: 2:3
Capital: Columbia
What it means: The palmetto is the state's official tree.

South Dakota

Adopted: 1963
Ratio: 3:5
Capital: Pierre
What it means: The state seal is depicted with the sun's rays around it. Among the elements featured in the seal are a farmer on his field, cattle, crops, a furnace and a steamship.

Tennessee

Adopted: 1905
Ratio: 3:5
Capital: Nashville
What it means: The design and colours are based on both the Confederate battle flag and the U.S. flag.

Texas

Adopted: 1839
Ratio: 2:3
Capital: Austin
What it means: The colours and the stripes are taken from the U.S. flag – blue for loyalty, white for strength, and red for bravery.

Utah

Adopted: 1913
Ratio: 2:3
Capital: Salt Lake City
What it means: 1847 was the year when the first Mormon settlers came to Salt Lake City. 1896 marked Utah's joining the Union as the 45th state. The beehive is symbolic of industry. Sego lilies, the state flower, stand for peace.

Vermont

Adopted: 1923
Ratio: 3:5
Capital: Montpelier
What it means: The coat of arms pictures the Green Mountains in the background, with a large pine tree, a cow and sheaves of wheat in the foreground. A stag's head is at the crest.

Virginia

Adopted: 1861
Ratio: 7:11
Capital: Richmond
What it means: The state seal features a woman dressed as an ancient warrior, wearing a helmet and holding a spear and sword. She is standing over the figure of a tyrant lying on the ground. The Latin motto reads: "Thus always to tyrants."

Washington

Adopted: 1923
Ratio: 2:3
Capital: Olympia
What it means: The state seal bears the name of the state, the date of admission into the Union, and a bust of George Washington, the first president of the U.S.A.

West Virginia

Adopted: 1929
Ratio: 10:19
Capital: Charleston
What it means: The seal has a farmer and a mountaineer standing on either side of a rock with the date when West Virginia was admitted into the Union.

Wisconsin

Adopted: 1913
Ratio: 2:3
Capital: Madison
What it means: The date recalls the attainment of statehood. The U.S. motto "One out of many" and the national shield are inscribed at the centre.

Wyoming

Adopted: 1917
Ratio: 2:3
Capital: Cheyenne
What it means: The white bison carries the 1893 state seal. The seal depicts a rancher and a miner. The woman represents equal rights.

District of Colombia

Adopted: 1938
Ratio: 10:19
Capital: Washington D.C.
What it means: The design was based on the shield from the coat of arms used by the Washington family.

CANADA

The northernmost country in North America, Canada also makes up nearly two-fifths of the continent. The country occupies an area of 9,984,670 square kilometres (3,855,103 square miles).

Alberta

Adopted: 1968
Ratio: 1:2
Capital: Edmonton
What it means: The St George Cross recalls the region's English settlement.

1 Yukon Territory
2 British Columbia
3 Northwest Territories
4 Alberta
5 Saskatchewan
6 Nunavut
7 Manitoba
8 Ontario
9 Quebec
10 Newfoundland and Labrador
11 Prince Edward Island
12 New Brunswick
13 Nova Scotia

British Columbia

Adopted: 1960
Ratio: 3:5
Capital: Victoria
What it means: Features an extended Union Jack in the upper half, with a golden crown at the centre.

Manitoba

Adopted: 1966
Ratio: 1:2
Capital: Winnipeg
What it means: The coat of arms bears a bison (a source of food and clothing) and the Cross of St George.

New Brunswick

Adopted: 1965
Ratio: 5:8
Capital: Fredericton
What it means: The golden lion in the upper red stripe is believed to recall the region's ties with England.

Newfoundland and Labrador

Adopted: 1980
Ratio: 1:2
Capital: Saint John's
What it means: The two red-outlined triangles represent the mainland and the islands.

Northwest Territories

Adopted: 1969
Ratio: 1:2
Capital: Yellowknife
What it means: Blue is symbolic of the skies and waters in the territory, and white of the ice and snow.

Nova Scotia

Adopted: 1929
Ratio: 3:4
Capital: Halifax
What it means: Based on the royal arms of Scotland and the Scottish St Andrew Cross (with the colours reversed).

Nunavut

Adopted: 1999
Ratio: 9:16
Capital: Iqaluit
What it means: The traditional inuksuk at the centre represents stone markers that guide people on land.

Ontario

Adopted: 1965
Ratio: 1:2
Capital: Toronto
What it means: This was the first flag in Canada to feature the maple leaf.

Prince Edward Island

Adopted: 1964
Ratio: 2:3
Capital: Charlottetown
What it means: Based on a banner featuring the 1905 coat of arms.

Quebec

Adopted: 1948
Ratio: 2:3
Capital: Québec City
What it means: Each of the quarters bear a fleur-de-lys (flowers), which has historic associations with France.

Saskatchewan

Adopted: 1962
Ratio: 1:2
Capital: Regina
What it means: The prairie lily is the official floral emblem of the province.

Yukon Territory

Adopted: 1967
Ratio: 1:2
Capital: Whitehorse
What it means: At the centre are the coat of arms and the territory's floral emblem.

UNITED KINGDOM

Great Britain – comprising England, Wales and Scotland – and Northern Ireland are together called the United Kingdom. It is an island country located off the northwestern coast of the European mainland. With the exception of the land border with the Republic of Ireland, the United Kingdom is surrounded by sea – the North Sea, the English Channel, the Celtic Sea, the Irish Sea and the Atlantic Ocean.

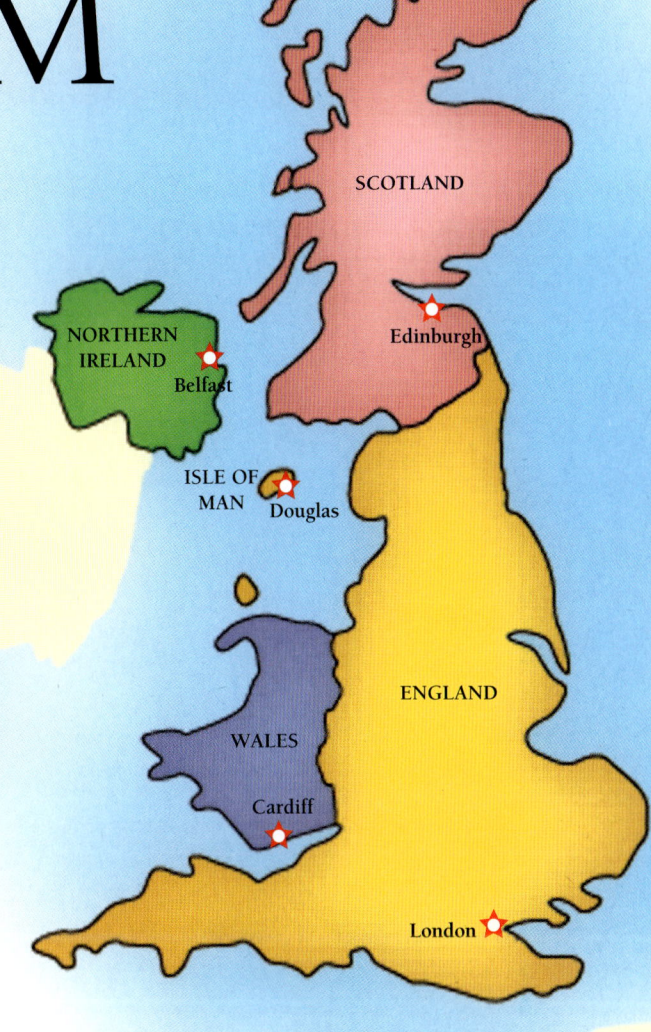

Alderney

Adopted: 1906
Ratio: 3:5
Capital: St Anne
What it means: Features the Cross of St George and the coat of arms.

England

Adopted: 1277
Ratio: 3:5
Capital: London
What it means: The Cross of St George is featured against a white field.

Guernsey

Adopted: 1962
Ratio: 2:3
Capital: St Peter Port
What it means: The gold cross sets it apart from the flag of England.

Isle of Man

Adopted in: 1971
Ratio: 1:2
Capital: Douglas
What it means: Features the symbol of triskelion, which is believed to be based on an ancient Sun symbol.

Jersey

Adopted: 1981
Ratio: 3:5
Capital: St Helier
What it means: The coat of arms and crown is featured at the top.

Northern Ireland

Adopted: 1953
Ratio: 1:2
Capital: Belfast
What it means: This flag ceased to be official in 1973. The Union Jack is currently used as the official flag.

Sark

Adopted: 1938
Ratio: 3:5
Capital: L'Ecluse
What it means: Incorporates the Cross of St George. The red canton features two yellow lions.

Scotland

Adopted: 1512
Ratio: 3:5
Capital: Edinburgh
What it means: The Cross of St Andrew is in honour of the patron saint of Scotland.

Wales

Adopted: 1959
Ratio: 3:5
Capital: Cardiff
What it means: The Red Dragon has long been an emblem for the Welsh people.

INTERNATIONAL
FLAGS

Arab League

Features the emblem of the league, which currently comprises 22 Arab states.

ASEAN

The flag of the Association of Southeast Asian Nations represents the main colours of the flags of the 10 member nations.

CARICOM

The yellow circle in the centre of the flag represents the sun, bearing the logo of the Caribbean Community and Common Market, founded in 1973.

CIS

The Commonwealth of Independent States is a confederation of 12 countries belonging to the former Soviet Union.

Commonwealth

The logo of the Commonwealth of Nations features the letter C about a representation of the globe.

European Union

The 12 gold stars symbolise the union of the peoples of European countries.

NATO

The North Atlantic Treaty Organization is an international defence alliance, meant chiefly for countries in Europe and North America.

OAS

The Organization of American States is an association of nearly all the independent countries in North America, Central America and South America

OAU (African Union)

The coat of arms is featured in the centre.

OIC

The flag of the Organization of the Islamic Conference features pan-Arab colours and the inscription 'Allahu Akbar', meaning 'God is great.'

Olympic Movement

The five interlocked rings were incorporated to represent the 'five parts of the world' in which the games were pursued actively.

OPEC

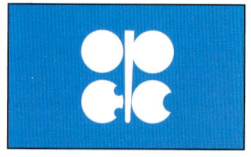

The Organization of Petroleum Exporting Countries was set up to coordinate petroleum-related policies of oil-producing nations.

Pacific Community

The stars stand for the member countries.

Red Cross

The International Movement of the Red Cross and Red Crescent is a humanitarian agency. Its flag features the well known symbols of mercy and complete neutrality.

United Nations

The flag depicts a map of the Earth flanked by two olive branches – an apt logo for a peacekeeping organisation.

SIGNAL FLAGS

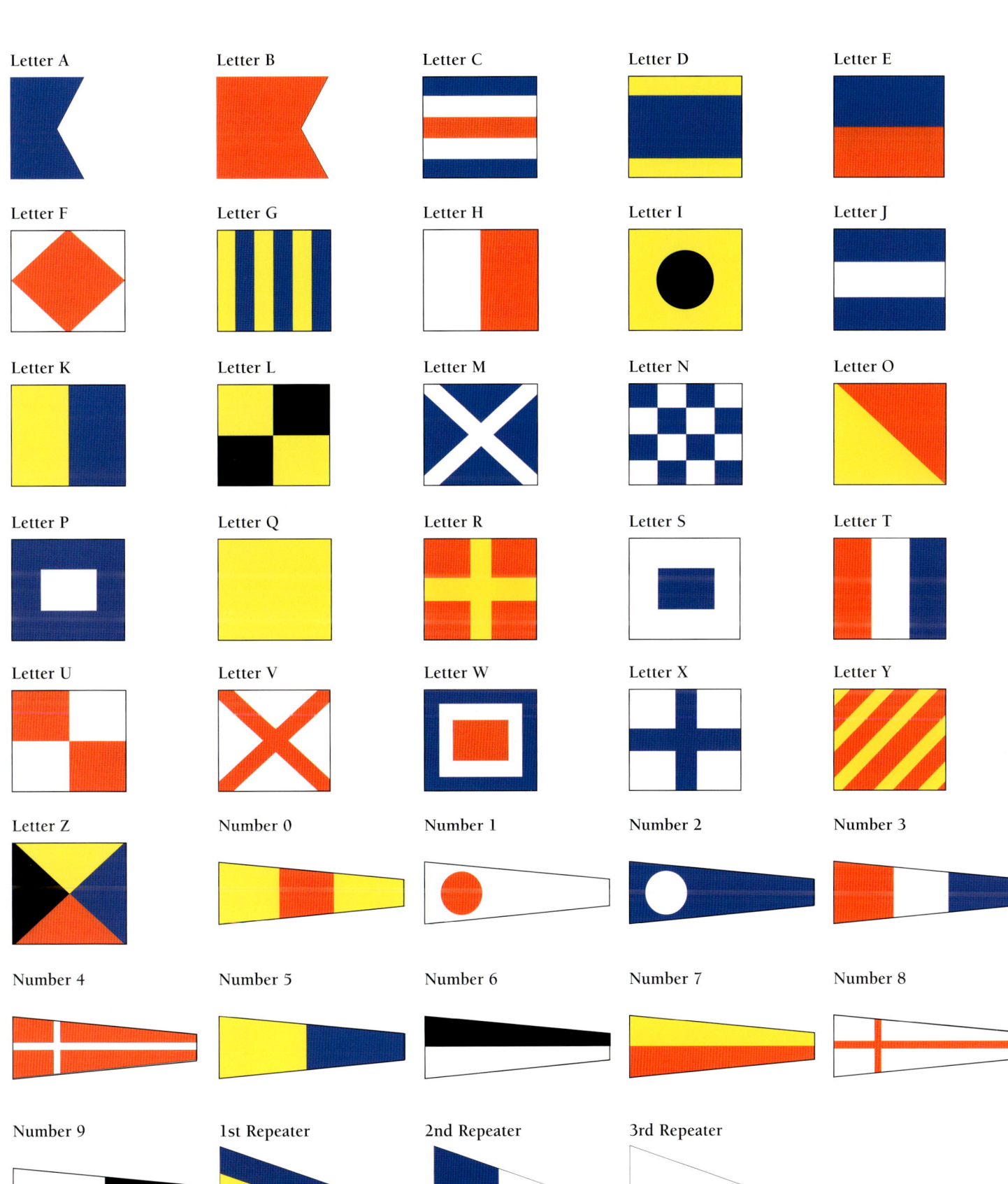

Letter A	Letter B	Letter C	Letter D	Letter E
Letter F	Letter G	Letter H	Letter I	Letter J
Letter K	Letter L	Letter M	Letter N	Letter O
Letter P	Letter Q	Letter R	Letter S	Letter T
Letter U	Letter V	Letter W	Letter X	Letter Y
Letter Z	Number 0	Number 1	Number 2	Number 3
Number 4	Number 5	Number 6	Number 7	Number 8
Number 9	1st Repeater	2nd Repeater	3rd Repeater	

TYPES OF FLAGS

Match the given type of flags on this page with the specific flags on the opposite page.
Find out which shapes and designs are more commonly used!

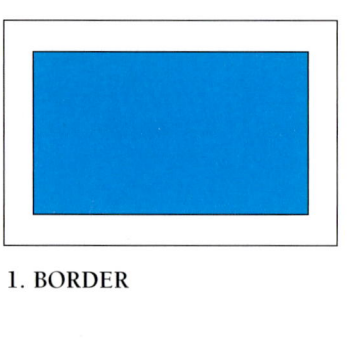

1. BORDER

2. BICOLOUR

3. SALTIRE

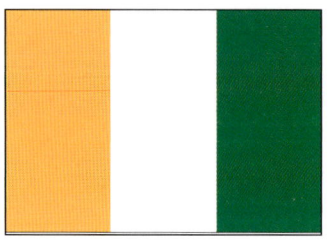

4. TRICOLOUR

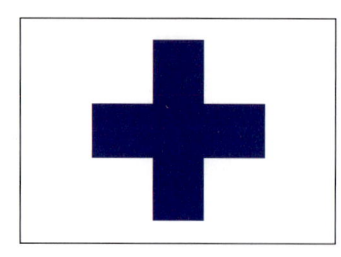

5. COUPED CROSS

6. CROSS

7. FIMBRIATION

8. SCANDINAVIAN CROSS

9. SERRATION

INDEX

90, 91

Burgos, Spain, 50 L3

Burkina Faso, Africa, 52 C11, 54 I7, 98, 99

Burma (Myanmar), Asia, 58 D13, 65 S6, 96, 97

Bursa, Turkey, 62 E2

Bydgoszcz, Poland, 48 C7

C

Cadiz, Spain, 50 I11

Cagliari, Sardinia, 46 K5

Cairns, Australia, 75 P5

California (State), U.S.A., 25 M9

Cambodia, Asia, 58 E14, 70 I8, 96

Cambrian Mts, U.K., 39 O9

Cameroon 98, 99

Campinas, Brazil, 33 N10

Canada 77, 80, 81, 106, 110

Canadian Shield, North America, 19 O7

Canary Islands, Atlantic Ocean, 51 T11, 52 I4,

Canberra, Australia, 75 P11

Cannes, France, 43 R11

Canterbury Plains, New Zealand, 76 G9

Cape Breton Island, Atlantic Ocean, 21 U12

Cape Howe, Australia, 73 P9

Cape Leeuwin, Australia, 72 K8

Cape Town, South Africa, 56 I12

Cape Verde 98, 99

Cape York Peninsula, Australia, 73 O5, 75 O3

Capri (Island), Mediterranean Sea, 46 I6

Caracas, Venezuela, 32 I2

Carbonia, Sardinia, 46 J4

Carribbean 77, 84, 85

Caribbean Sea, 19, 29, 31, 32,

Carlisle, U.K., 38 L10

Carpathian Mts, Europe, 37 Q8, 48 I9, 88

Carpentaria, Gulf of, Australia, 73 N4, 75 M3

Carson City, U.S.A., 25 M10

Cartagena, Spain, 51 O9

Casablanca, Morocco, 54 H2

Cascade Range (Mts), U.S.A., 25 M7

Caspian Sea, Asia-Europe, 37, 58, 60, 62

Catania, Sicily, 47 M10

Caucasus (Mts), Asia-Europe, 37 V8, 58 K5, 90

Cayman Islands 84

Cebu (Island), Philippines, 71 N9

Celebes Island, Indonesia, 59 T11, 71 M12

Celebes Sea, 59, 71, 72

Celtic Sea, 39, 111

Central Asian Uplands, Asia, 58 K4

Central Russian Uplands, Europe, 37 S5

Central Siberian Plateau, Asia, 59 Q2

Chad 28

Changsha, China, 67 O12

Channel Islands, English Channel, 36 B13, 39 S9

Charismas Island, Indian Ocean, 70 I15

Charleston (South Carolina), U.S.A., 27 S4

Charleston (West Virginia), U.S.A., 23 N13

Charlotte, U.S.A., 27 R3

Chattahoochee (River), U.S.A., 27 P5

Chattanooga, U.S.A., 27 P3

Chelyabinsk, Rus. Fed., 61 M7

Cheyenne, U.S.A., 25 Q9

Chicago, U.S.A., 22 J11

Chile, South America, 30 D13, 34 G6, 82, 83

China, Asia, 58 D13, 66, 77, 78

Chisinau, Moldova, 60 E6

Christchurch, New Zealand, 76 H9

Chu (River), Asia, 59 N5

Chudskoye Lake, Europe, 37 Q4

Chukchi Sea, 16

Cincinnati, U.S.A., 22 L13

Cleveland, U.S.A., 23 M11

Coast Mts, Canada, 20 I12

Coastal Plains, North America, 19 O11

Cocos Islands, Indian Ocean, 70 P15

Colombia, South America, 30 D10, 32 G4, 81, 82, 83

Colombo, Sri lanka, 65 M12

Colorado (River), U.S.A., 26 I6

Colorado (State), U.S.A., 25 N13

Columbia (City), U.S.A., 25 N6

Columbus (Georgia), U.S.A., 27 P4

Columbus (Ohio), U.S.A., 23 L13

Comoros Islands, Indian Ocean, 53 R11, 57 O6, 102, 103

Concord, U.S.A., 23 R9

Congo Basin, Africa, 53 O10, 100

Connecticut (State), U.S.A., 23 R10

Constance Lake, Europe, 43 S8

Constanta, Romania, 48 J12

Cook Strait, New Zealand, 73 S10, 76 I7

Coral Sea Islands, Pacific Ocean, 72 E12

Coral Sea, Australia, 73, 75

Cordoba, Spain, 50 J9

Coromandel Coast, India, 65 M10

Corpus Christi, U.S.A., 26 I8

Corrientes, Argentina, 34 E10

Corsica (Island), Mediterranean Sea, 43 R12, 46 G5

Costa Brava , Spain, 51 S3

Costa Dorada, Spain, 51 R4

Costa Rica, North America, 18 F15, 29 O11

Crete (Island), Mediterranean Sea, 37 Q12, 49 P10

Crimea (Island), Europe, 37 S8

Croatia 90, 91

Cuba (Island), Caribbean Sea, 18 F14, 19 R13, 29 P7, 84

Cumbrian Mts, U.K., 39 L9

Cyclades Islands, Mediterranean Sea, 49 O10

Cyprus (Island), Mediterranean Sea, 37 S12, 62 E3, 92

Cyprus, Asia, 58 B12

Czech Republic 88, 89

D

Dakar, Senegal, 54 D7

Dakhla, Western Sahara, 54 E4

Dallas, U.S.A., 26 J4

Damascus, Syria, 62 G4

Dar-es-Salaam, Tanzania, 57 O4

Darling (River), Australia, 73 O7, 75 O9

Darwin, Australia, 74 K3

Davao, Philippines, 71 N10

Davis Mts, U.S.A., 26 E6

Davis Sea, 17

Davis Strait, North America, 16 D8, 19 Q4, 21 R9

Delaware (State), U.S.A., 23 Q13

Denmark 80, 96, 98, 99

Denver, U.S.A., 25 S10

Des Moines (River), U.S.A., 22 G12

Des Moines(City), U.S.A., 22 F12

Detroit, U.S.A., 22 L11

Dhaka, Bangladesh, 65 P6

Di Bolsena Lake, Italy, 46 G8

Diego Saurez, Madagascar, 57 Q6

Dili, Timor, Asia, 71 N14

Disappointment Lake, Australia, 72 K6, 74 H6

Djibouti 100, 101

Dnepropetrovsk, Ukraine, 60 G7

Dniester (River), Europe, 37 Q7, 60 E4

Dodecanese Islands, Mediterranean Sea, 49 O11

Dominica (Island), Caribbean Sea, Dominica, 19 G14, 29 V7 84, 85

Dominican Republic (Island), Caribbean Sea, 19 G14, 29 V7, 84

Don (River), Rus. Fed., 37 T7, 58 K5, 60 K7

Donetsk, Ukraine, 60 G8

Dongola, Sudan, 55 P6

Dordrecht, The Netherlands, 44 L10

Douglas, U.K., 39 L8

Dover, Strait of, Europe, 39 Q13

Dover, U.S.A., 23 Q12

Drakensberg Mts, Africa, 53 P14

Drava (River), Croatia-Slovenia, 48 H6

Dresden, Germany, 43 U5

Duero (River), Spain, 36 J8, 51 L4

Duluth, U.S.A., 22 G8

Durban, South Africa, 56 L10

Dushanbe, Tajikistan, 61 L10

Dusseldorf, Germany, 43 R4

Dvina (River), Europe, 37 S3

E

East China Sea, 59, 67, 69

East Siberian Mts, Asia, 59 S2

East Siberian Sea, 16

East Timor, Asia, 58 F15, 71 O14, 96

Eastern Ghats (Mts), India, 59 O10

Eastmain (River), Canada,

19 Q8

Ebro (River), Spain, 36 L9, 51 N4

Ecuador, South America, 30 C11, 32 F5, 82, 83

El Paso, U.S.A., 26 E5

Eindhoven, The Netherlands, 45 L12

Egypt 93, 100, 101

El Fasher, Sudan, 55 O7

El Obeid, Sudan, 55 P7

El Paso, U.S.A., 25 R14

El Salvador, North America, 18 E14, 29 M10, 80, 81

Elba (Island), Mediterranean Sea, 46 F6

Elbe (River), Europe, 37 O7, 43 S3

Elbert (Mts), U.S.A., R10

Elbrus Mt, Rus. Fed., 37 U9, 60 J7

Elburz Mts, Iran, 63 L3

Ellesmere Island, Arctic Ocean, 16 G6, 21 N6

Emi Koussi (Mts), Chad, 55 M6

English Channel, Europe, 36 L6, 37 M6, 39 R10, 111

Enschede, The Netherlands, 44 J14

Equatorial Guinea 98, 99

Erie Lake, Canada-U.S.A., 19 Q9, 21 Q15, 23 M11

Eritrea, Africa, 52 F11, 55 S6, 100, 101

Esbjerg, Denmark, 40 J14

Esfahan, Iran, 62 L5

Essen, Germany, 43 R4

Estonia, Europe, 36 D12, 60 I2, 90, 91

Ethiopia, Africa, 52 F12, 55 S9, 100, 101

Ethiopian Highlands, Africa, 53 Q8

Etna, Mt Sicily, 47 L10

Eugene, U.S.A., 25 L7

Euphrates (River), Iraq, 58 J6, 62 H3

Everest Mt, Nepal-China, 59 P8, 65 O4

Eyre Lake, Australia, 73 N7, 75 M9

F

Faeroe Islands, Denmark, 36 C11

Faial (Island), Atlantic Ocean, 51 R8

Fairbanks, U.S.A., 20 H9

Falklands Islands, Atlantic Ocean, 30 D14, 31 O14, 34 J13, 82, 83

Falum, Sweden, 41 N12

Fargo, U.S.A., 25 U7

Fed. States of Micronesia,

Montpelier, U.S.A., 23 Q9
Montreal, Canada, 21 S14
Morocco 99, 100
Moroni, Comoros, 57 O6
Moscow, Rus. Fed., 60 K5
Moshi, Tanzania N4 57
Mosul, Iraq, 62 I3
Mount Isa, Australia, 75 M6
Mozambique 100, 102, 103
Mulhouse, France, 43 Q8
Mull (Island), Atlantic Ocean, 38 J8
Murchison (River), Australia, 74 F8
Murcia, Spain, 51 O9
Murmansk, Rus. Fed., 61 M4
Murrray (River), Australia, 73 O8, 75 O11
Murrumbidgee (River), Australia, 75 O11
Muscat, Oman, 63 N8
Musgrave Ranges (Mts), Australia, 74 K8

N

N. Dvina (River), Asia, 59 L3
Nagasaki, Japan, 69 O7
Namib Desert, Namibia, 52 N13, 56 H8, 103
Namsos, Norway, 41 M8
Nantes, France, 43, L8
Nashville, U.S.A., 27 O2
Nassau, Bahamas, 29 P5
Nasser Lake, Egypt, 55 Q4, 53
Natal, South Africa, 56 K10
Nauru (Island), Pacific Ocean, 72 F11
Nebraska (State), U.S.A., 25 T9
Nejd, Saudi Arabia, 62 G7
Nelson (River), Canada, 19 O6, 21 N12
Nelson, New Zealand, 76 H7
Nepal, Asia, 58 D13, 65 N4, 79, 94, 95
Netherlands Antilles (Islands), Caribbean Sea, 29 U9
Netherlands, The 86, 87
Nevada (State), U.S.A., 25 N10
New Britain (Island), Papua New Guinea, 74 F2
New Brunswick (Province), Canada, 21 S13
New Caledonia (Islands), Pacific Ocean, 72 E13, 73 R6
New Hampshire (State),

U.S.A., 23 R9
New Jersey (State), U.S.A., 23 Q11
New Mexico (State), U.S.A., 25 R13
New Orleans, U.S.A., 27 M6
New South Wales (State), Australia, 75 O10
New York (City), U.S.A., 23 Q11
New York (State), U.S.A., 23 P10
New Zealand, Australasia, 72 F14, 76, 104, 105
Newcastle-upon-Tyne, U.K., 38 L10
Newfoundland Island, Atlantic Ocean, 19 T6, 21 T11
Niagara Falls, Canada-U.S.A., 23 O10
Nicaragua 81
Nicobar Islands, Indian Ocean, 65 Q11
Nicosia, Cyprus, 62 F3
Niger 99
Nigeria 99
Niihau (Island), Pacific Ocean, 24 E5
Nijmegen, The Netherlands, 44 K12
Nis, Serbia & Montenegro, 48 J8
Nizhniy Novgorod, Rus. Fed., 60 L6
North America 80
North Atlantic 80
North Carolina (State), U.S.A., 27 S2
North Dakota (State), U.S.A., 25 T7
North European Plains, Europe, 37 Q6
North Island, Pacific Ocean, 73 T9, 76 H4
North Korea, Asia, 58 E12, 68 G6
North Sea, 37, 38, 40, 44, 111
North Uist (Island), Atlantic Ocean, 38 H7
Northern Mariana (Islands), Pacific Ocean, 72 D9
Northern Territory (Territory), Australia, 74 L5
Northwest Highlands, U.K., 38 H8
Northwest Territories (Province), Canada, 21 L10
Norway 88, 89
Norwegian Sea, 16, 37, 41
Nova Scotia (Province),

Canada, 19 S7, 21 T13
Novaya Zemlya (Island), Rus. Fed., 59 N1, 61 N4
Novi Sad, Serbia & Montenegro, 48 I8
Novosibirsk, Rus. Fed., 61 O8
Novosibirskiye Ostrova (Island), Arctic Ocean, 59 O2, 61 S4
Nubian Desert, Sudan, 53 P6, 55 Q5
Nullarbor Plain, Australia, 73 L8
Nyasa Lake, Malawi-Mozambique, 53 Q11, 57 M6

O

Oahu (Island), Pacific Ocean, 24 F6
Ob (River), Rus. Fed., 37 V1, 59 N3, 61 N6
Oceania 104
Odense, Denmark, 40 K15
Odesa, Ukraine, 60 E7
Ogaden Desert, Africa, 53 R8
Ohio (River), U.S.A., 19 Q9, 22 I15
Ohio (State), U.S.A., 23 L12
Okhotsk, Sea of, 59, 61, 68
Oki Islands, Pacific Ocean, 68 K8
Oklahoma (State), U.S.A., 25 V12
Oklahoma City, U.S.A., 25 V12
Oland (Island), Sweden, 41 N14
Olympia, U.S.A., 25 M6
Olympus Mt, Greece, 49 L9
Oman, Asia, 58 B13, 63 M9, 92, 93
Omsk, Rus. Fed., 61 N8
Onega, Europe, 37 S3
Ontario Lake, Canada-U.S.A., 23 O9
Orange (River), South Africa, 53 N14, 56 I10
Orebro, Sweden, 41 M12
Oregon (State), U.S.A., 25 M8
Oristano, Sardinia, 46 J5
Orkney (Islands), Atlantic Ocean, 38 G9
Orlando, U.S.A., 27 R7
Orleans, France, 43 N8
Osaka, Japan, 69 M10
Ostende, Belgium, 45 M7
Osumi (Islands), Pacific Ocean, 69 Q7
Otranto, Strait of, Italy, 46 H12
Ouagadougou, Burkina Faso, 54 I8

P

Padang, Indonesia, 70 G12
Pakistan, Asia, 58 C13, 64 I4, 94, 95
Palau (Islands), Pacific Ocean, 72 C10, 104, 105
Palermo, Sicily, 47 L9
Palma, Mallorca, 51 S6
Palu, Indonesia, 71 M12
Pampas, Argentina, 31 O11, 34 I9
Pamplona, Spain, 51 N2
Panama 81
Pantelleria (Island), Mediterranean Sea, 47 N7
Papua New Guinea, Australasia, 71 T13, 72 D12, 73 O3, 74 E2, 105
Paraguay (Country), South America, 30 E12, 34 C9, 82, 83
Paramaribo, Suriname, 32 L3
Paris, France, 43 N7
Patagonia, South America, 31 N13, 34 L7
Pearl (River), U.S.A., 26 M5
Pecos (River), U.S.A., 26 G6
Pennines (Mts), U.K., 38 L10
Pennsylvania (State), U.S.A., 23 O12
Perm, Rus. Fed., 61 M7
Persian Gulf, Asia, 58 K7, 62 K6
Perth, Australia, 74 G10
Pertopavlovsk-Kamchatskiy, Rus. Fed., 61 W6
Peru, South America, 30 C11, 32 F8, 82, 83
Pescara, Italy, 46 G10
Petropavlovsk, Rus. Fed., 61 N8
Philadelphia, U.S.A., 23 Q12
Philippine Sea, 47, 59
Philippines, Asia, 58 F14, 71 N8, 96, 97
Phoenix, U.S.A., 25 P13
Pico (Island), Atlantic Ocean, 51 S9
Pierre, U.S.A., 25 T8
Pisa, Italy, 46 E7
Pittsburgh, U.S.A., 23 N12
Plains of Hungary, Europe, 37 P9
Poland 88, 89
Polynesia 104
Ponta Delgada, Azores, 51 R9

Pontianak, Indonesia, 70 J12
Pontic (Mts), Turkey, 62 H2
Port Augusta, Australia, 75 M10
Port Elizabeth, South Africa, 56 K11
Port Hedland, Australia, 74 G6
Port Moresby, Papua New Guinea, 74 F3
Port Said, Egypt, 55 Q3
Port Sudan, Sudan, 55 R6
Portland, U.S.A., 25 M6
Portsmouth, U.K., 39 Q11
Portugal 83, 87, 96, 98, 99
Prespa Lake, Macedonia-Greece, 48 L8
Preston, U.K., 39 M10
Pretoria, South Africa, 56 K10
Prince Edward Island (Province), Canada, 21 T12
Providence, U.S.A., 23 S10
Puerto Rico (Island), Caribbean Sea, 18 G14, 29 T7, 84, 85
Punta Arenas, Chile, 35 P8
Purus (River), Brazil, 31 N6, 32 J6
Putumayo (River), South America, 31 M6
Pyrenees (Mts), France-Spain, 36 L9, 43 N12, 51 O3

Q

Qatar, Asia, 58 B13, 62 L7, 92, 93
Quebec (City), Canada, 21 S13
Queen Charlotte (Islands), Pacific Ocean, 18 K6, 20 H12
Queen Elizabeth (Islands), Arctic Ocean, 16 E6, 21 M7
Queensland (State), Australia, 75 N7

R

Ragusa, Sicily, 47 N10
Raleigh, U.S.A., 27 S2
Ras Dashen (Mt), Ethiopia, 55 S7
Red (River), Asia, 70 I5
Red Sea, 52, 53, 55, 58, 62
Regensburg, Germany, 43 U7
Reims, France, 43 O7
Rennes, France, 43 L8

ARCTIC OCE

GREENLAND
(DENMARK)

ICELAND
Faeroe Islands
(DENMARK)

CIRCLE

ALASKA
(USA)

IRELAND
UNITED
KINGD

CANADA

Aleutian Islands
(USA)

ATLANTIC OCEAN

Azores
(PORTUGAL)

PORTUGAL
SPAI

PACIFIC OCEAN

UNITED STATES OF AMERICA

Madeira
(PORTUGAL)
Gibraltar
(UK)

MOROCCO

TROPIC OF CANCER

MEXICO

BAHAMAS

Canary
Islands
(SPAIN)

WESTERN
SAHARA

Hawaiian
Islands (USA)

CUBA
DOMINICAN
REPUBLIC

MAURITANIA

Cape
Verde

BELIZE
JAMAICA
HAITI
13

2
4

GUATEMALA
HONDURAS
EL SALVADOR
NICARAGUA

CARIBBEAN
SEA

5
6
8

SENEGAL
GAMBIA
GUINEA-BISSAU
GUINEA

Ile Clipperton
(FRANCE)

COSTA
RICA
PANAMA

U 12
9
10

SIERRA LEONE
LIBERIA
IVORY
COAST

BURK
FAS

Kiritimati
(KIRIBATI)

Coco Island
(COSTA RICA)

VENEZUELA

GUYANA
SURINAM
FRENCH GUIANA

EQUATOR

COLOMBIA

EQUATOR

Galapagos
Islands
(ECUADOR)

ECUADOR

Marquesas Islands
(FR POLY)

PERU

BRAZIL

Tuamotu
Islands
(FR POLY)

BOLIVIA

FRENCH
POLYNESIA

Pitcairn (UK)

TROPIC OF CAPRICORN

Isla San
Ambrosio
(CHILE)

PARAGUAY

Easter Island
(CHILE)

CHILE

Archipelago
Juan Fernandez
(CHILE)

ARGENTINA

URUGUAY

Falkland
Islands
(UK)

South Georgia (UK)

ANTARCTIC CIRCLE